STRANGER ON EARTH

BOOKS BY RICHARD JONES

May 2019

STRANGER ON EARTH

RICHARD JONES

*For Susan —
As I know you will
appreciate the
Beauty.

Much love, Richard*

COPPER CANYON PRESS
PORT TOWNSEND, WASHINGTON

Cover art: Cover art: Francis Picabia, *Parade Amoureuse*
© 2017 Artists Rights Society (ARS), New York / ADAGP, Paris

Copper Canyon Press is in residence at Fort Worden State Park in Port
Townsend, Washington, under the auspices of Centrum. Centrum is a gathering
place for artists and creative thinkers from around the world, students of all ages
and backgrounds, and audiences seeking extraordinary cultural enrichment.

LIBRARY OF CONGRESS CATALOGING-IN-PUBLICATION DATA
Names: Jones, Richard, 1953– author.
Title: Stranger on Earth / Richard Jones.
Description: Port Townsend, Washington : Copper Canyon Press, [2018]
Identifiers: LCCN 2018000790 | ISBN 9781556595356
(softcover : acid-free paper)
Classification: LCC PS3560.O52475 A6 2018 | DDC 811/.54—dc23
LC record available at https://lccn.loc.gov/2018000790

98765432 FIRST PRINTING

COPPER CANYON PRESS
Post Office Box 271
Port Townsend, Washington 98368
www.coppercanyonpress.org

for Sarah & William & Andrew & Laura—
my fellow travelers

For the sake of a single verse, one must see many cities,
men, and things, one must know the animals, one must feel
how the birds fly and know the gesture with which the little
flowers open in the morning. One must be able to think back
to roads in unknown regions, to unexpected meetings
and to partings one had long seen coming; to days
of childhood that are still unexplained, to parents whom
one had to hurt when they brought one some joy and one did not
grasp it (it was a joy for someone else); to childhood illnesses
that so strangely begin with such a number of profound
and grave transformations, to days in rooms withdrawn
and quiet and to mornings by the sea, to the sea itself, to seas,
to nights of travel that rushed along on high and flew with all
the stars—and it is not yet enough if one may think of all this.
One must have memories of many nights of love, none of
which was like the others, of the screams of women in labor,
and of light, white, sleeping women in childbed, closing again.
But one must also have been beside the dying, must have sat
beside the dead in the room with the open window and the
fitful noises. And still it is not enough to have memories.
One must be able to forget them when they are many,
and one must have the great patience to wait until they come
again. For it is not yet the memories themselves. Not till
they have turned to blood within us, to glance and gesture,
nameless and no longer to be distinguished from ourselves—
not till then can it happen that in a most rare hour
the first word of a verse arises in their midst
and goes forth from them.

RAINER MARIA RILKE

CONTENTS

SIX: THE ITALIAN CANTOS

STRANGER ON EARTH

1

PAVILION WAY

The land on which we live
once had the highly poetic privilege
of being the end of the world.

G.K. CHESTERTON,
A Short History of England

The Silver Cord

Apparently I was not keen to be born.
Three weeks late,
I refused to come into the world;
my mother could only lie in her hospital bed
and wait. "Meaningless! Meaningless!"
cries the teacher of Ecclesiastes,
and I fancy myself there in my mother's womb
pondering those words about life and existence.
That year in England my father had flown
to Spain, Germany, Italy, and Egypt.
He flew to other countries, also—
he had a special passport from the Embassy
that allowed him to fly to Portugal,
where he enjoyed secret adventures he never shared,
wild stories lost forever,
now that he's gone to his grave.
The teacher of Ecclesiastes says
the former generations will not be remembered
by those to come
and says to remember the Creator each day
before the silver cord is severed
and the golden bowl is broken.
That long-ago August,
as I declined the world's golden invitation,
my father's father lay dying in Virginia.
My father did not know whether to stay in London
and wait to celebrate my birth
or fly to America and mourn.
After I was born, he went home—too late.
It was the same for me. The day the call came

that my father was near death,
I crossed the country to his home by the ocean,
yet when I arrived
he was already laid in his coffin.
It must have hurt him greatly
not to fly across the vast blue-and-gray nothingness
of the Atlantic; it must have hurt
not to sit by his father and say goodbye,
not to kiss the dying hand.

The Coronation

1953

My uncomfortably pregnant mother
and my father and sister,
and I, too, I guess,
at my leisure resting unborn inside my mother's belly,
stood with England
as Her Royal Highness the Princess
rode by in the Gold State Coach.
My father had guaranteed a viewing spot
by spending a cold night along the route.
The coach drove slowly from
Buckingham Palace to Westminster Abbey
as the Princess's subjects cheered
and my father lifted his camera
and took the most marvelous portrait.
Drawn by eight horses with a postilion
and accompanied by grooms, footmen,
and red and gold Yeomen of the Guard,
the gold coach comes near,
blessed by golden angels on the roof
and guarded by four gold Tritons
trumpeting glory to the ends of the earth.
Elizabeth leans toward the camera,
nodding her head to our family
and me, dreamily floating in my mother's womb.
I wonder whether I heard the gun salutes
fired from the Tower of London
or felt the concussion of fireworks
exploding over Victoria Embankment.
My father believed I could hear his voice

when at home he'd put his hand on my mother's stomach
and talk to me. As the tenth month approached,
he'd daily request that I "make an appearance."
After the coronation,
my sister in her tartan skirt and navy blazer
would come home from school
and lie in my mother's lap
to tell me about the scepter and cross,
Edward's crown,
the Sovereign's Orb and Ring,
the eagle-shaped vase with the anointing oil.
She'd say "God Save the Queen"
and run off to play by herself
in the keep of some high-towered imaginary castle.

The Eighth Day

Eight days after I was born,
my mother and father wrapped me in swaddling clothes,
placed me in a black pram,
and strolled down Pavilion Way to Dr. Lambert's,
our Jewish doctor and friend,
where at a small celebration in his home
I was circumcised on the kitchen table.
In my mind I have tried to picture the holy knife
and the friendly doctor
and the happy party gathered around me.
Over the course of a lifetime,
I've needed paintings by the masters
to guide my vision of that day in London.
Our family doctor looks like the bearded rabbi
in Luca Signorelli's *The Circumcision*.
The French *Book of Hours* helps me see
my mother, watching like young Mary.
The bearded English neighbor, like Joseph,
lifts his hands to God. And above me,
in place of the kitchen's cold overhead light,
Peter Paul Rubens's heaven reveals itself
and makes known a chorus of music-making angels
illumined by a burning, golden, radiant glory—
the true circumcision of the spirit.
Paintings by Albrecht Dürer, Giovanni Bellini,
Fra Angelico, Parmigianino, and Mantegna
have taken me so deep into suspect memories
that I now blur the lines between
the eternities of earth and heaven.
In the doctor's kitchen, my father

places a drop of wine in my mouth.
Champagne glasses clink toasts "to life"
and blessings are spoken over my new heart.
The pipe and cigarette smoke
is as thick and blue as incense
in the temple of ancient Jerusalem,
so when Dr. Lambert's elderly, white-haired father
lifts my tiny body and holds me in his arms
I confuse Welsh drinking songs
with Simeon's farewell to the world—
the canticle of the Nunc Dimittis.

Gliders

Between tours of duty that took my father
around the world and down into hell,
he stole three weeks' R&R in Florida,
needing comfort and consolation from the War
and from all his eyes had seen.
An Army Air Corp C-47 pilot
who flew the Hump in the Burma Theater,
he was then assigned to the Laurinburg–Maxton
Army Air Base in North Carolina,
the world's largest glider pilot training program.
The gliders were not like the small
sleek gliders flown by amateurs today,
but huge unpowered aircraft.
The gliders could hold a dozen troops,
jeeps, mortars, bazookas, machine guns, and ammunition.
My father in his C-47 towed the gliders down the runway
and into the air, where young pilots
practiced tank hunting or nighttime landings.
Or, more dangerously,
my father would swing down low,
like the chariot that came for Elijah,
and snatch the gliders off the ground with trick wires,
gliders that in real battle
would be loaded with wounded men
now caught up in the air to safety.
Perhaps in the great bird of his plane
he felt like the Lord, rapturing his people.
Once, my father spoke of a day
when his practice flight had been scrubbed.
A second crew—

his buddies from the tar-paper barracks—
took his plane up instead. My father remembered
standing on the airfield, helpless
as he looked into the sky
and saw the engines smoke and fail,
the heavy plane careering down,
the great explosion.
After the War, the base closed
and quickly became a ghost town,
the only building left standing
the Skyway Baptist Church.
But before the pilots disbanded,
my father met my mother,
a secretary who typed the papers for soldiers
headed to North Africa or Normandy or Italy.
The two slow-danced together at the base club
on a Saturday night in August.

Portraits

In London my sister was my father's
favorite subject to photograph.
He has a picture of her
talking to a bobby in Trafalgar Square.
Standing at attention at Windsor Castle
beside a soldier of the Queen's Guard
in his red coat and tall bearskin cap.
By the Thames pointing to Big Ben.
Posting a letter at a red letter box;
peeking out from a red phone booth.
At her one-room schoolhouse,
she stands in her school uniform—
blue blazer with heraldic patch,
blue-green tartan skirt,
black knee socks, saddle shoes,
and a straw hat with a long, blue ribbon.
There is a photograph of her
so young it breaks my heart,
waiting with our mother for a red double-decker bus
near Piccadilly, both of them wearing
fancy hats, smart outfits, and elegant gloves.
When I was little,
my father took pictures of us together—
my sister pushing my pram on Pavilion Way
and later the two of us playing in the snow at Cape Cod
or scavenging the rocky shore along the Bay of Fundy.
In childhood portraits, I, too, am nattily attired,
sometimes decked out with six-shooters,
chaps, pointy boots, kerchief,
and red straw cowboy hat,

and other times dressed to the nines
in gray suit and black tie,
my hair slicked back and shining,
a look of nonchalance on my face
as I gaze off into the future.
I am often pictured mid-stride,
stepping beyond the frame toward some great blessing.
Once I learned to walk, the camera could see
I had somewhere urgent and important to go.

The Aladdin Blue Flame Heater

We heated the house on Pavilion Way
with an Aladdin Blue Flame heater.
The metal heater—
pale green, slender, and light—
had a long handle with a coiled grip
so my father could move it from cold room
to cold room. The Aladdin heater
stood on four delicate feet
and its flame radiated
a faintly intoxicating incense.
With its one round, glass window
like an all-seeing eye,
it had the habitually wary countenance
of those protective *nazar* amulets
that ward off evil.
The tall chimney stood at attention,
a sentinel stoically keeping watch.
Whenever the flame died,
my father would fill the heater with kerosene
and then unlatch the chimney
and let it fall to the side.
With his silver lighter,
he'd light the circular wick,
tilt the chimney back until it locked,
and then look through the round window
and adjust the wick by turning a knob
until he had a perfectly safe,
round, blue flame.
My father was like a high priest in the temple

burning an offering of incense.
I wonder whether,
as an infant,
I stood wide-eyed in my crib,
contemplating the crown of blue fire.
All I know is that my father said
the Aladdin blue flame heater
was an altar of warmth and light,
a little god that kept us from the cold.
And England was always cold.

Fog

On Saturday nights
my mother and father left my sister and me
in the care of our German nanny.
My parents went to the theater—
my father in his tweed suit,
my mother in a black dress,
pearls, and white kid gloves.
They'd drive to the station,
park the big American DeSoto,
and take the train into town to dine.
Those years in London
they saw every show that opened—
Guys and Dolls with Vivian Blaine,
Carousel, Paint Your Wagon, Show Boat,
South Pacific with Mary Martin,
The King and I, and *Porgy and Bess*
with William Warfield and Leontyne Price.
One night after seeing Cole Porter's *Can-Can*
they returned home on the train
and when they came up from the Tube
it was impossible to see.
The greenish-yellow, thick-as-mud,
dangerous, and impenetrable fog
the Brits call "pea soup" had settled in.
Somehow in the blinding veils of vapor
they found the DeSoto.
My father, the pilot, disappeared behind the wheel
and started the engine.
My mother in her finery turned up her collar
and began walking in front of the car,

navigating through the fog
by tapping the curb with her foot
as her hand tapped on the DeSoto's front fender—
showing my father the way.
My mother's white-gloved hand reached
into the unknown;
the car crept forward by inches.
When the curb came to an end,
the big car and my mother
crossed a sea of mist.
Those long moments of oblivion,
they tell me,
were traveled by faith.
Then they were on Pavilion Way,
our little street of row houses.
In the blinding fog my mother counted the gates
of the white picket fences lining the lane—
one, two, three, four, five, six, seven—
until she came to our house,
where my sister was waiting in the window
and I was asleep in my crib.

The Garden

My father bought our food
from the outdoor market,
makeshift tents and tables
that lined the street at the village center
where cheese was cut from rounds with wire
and sugar was measured and weighed.
Our neighbor, Doris Shirley, with little success
counseled my father to eat like a Brit—
jellied eel and pork pie.
Mrs. Shirley was a gardener.
The English believe in gardens and walking
and fresh air. On clear days when
my father and Mrs. Shirley walked to the market,
he'd park my pram in the Shirleys' garden.
Black as night, the pram rode high
on four tall, silver wheels,
a soft cab of white linen,
and a canopy that towered overhead,
protecting from wind and rain.
My sister kept an eye on me,
pushing the pram around the garden
and naming all the flowers,
names Mrs. Shirley had printed
on wooden pegs pushed into the ground.
Now that I'm old I try to visit
my sister in Virginia twice a year.
When on a warm summer evening
we walk the stone paths that wind through her yard
past sweeping beds of color,
my white-haired sister points to the silver nameplates—

an orange and red daylily called *Outrageous,*
a pristine white iris called *Immortality.*
From all her letters
faithfully written and sent over the years,
I recognize the distinctive handwriting,
a charming cursive that moves me to see.
My sister still praises Mrs. Shirley for her aesthetics,
and says she models her own garden,
with its herbaceous borders and banks of flowers,
on that early inspiration from many years ago
when we were young,
our Eden.

The Races

Weekends my father drove west into the countryside
and watched the steeplechase races.
He'd park his big American DeSoto on lawns
festooned with white tents and picnickers,
and take pictures of the wooded hills and hedgerows,
the long, green meadows and fences.
He'd bought his Leica in Germany
and in his hands
the camera was a good camera for landscapes.
In his photographs, the horses and their riders
look small beneath the English sky,
which seems ominous and threatening.
He'd take pictures of the people, too,
ladies with parasols and men in straw hats
cheering on the perilous race.
My father had a good eye
and knew how to frame a scene,
his photographs as crisp and clean
as the photographs I've seen
in books and museums.
My father took these weekend trips on his own,
my mother preferring the pleasures of home.
He liked the glamour of the races,
the air of danger that hung over the fields,
the bravery of horse and rider.
She liked the company of a good book.
She'd make tea and sit by the window, reading.
The windows were covered by a lovely lace
my father brought my mother
as a housewarming gift from Belgium,

and the pattern of vines and leaves and flowers
burned white in the English sun
and let in a soft, diffused light.
We had only a few things back then,
and I still have my father's camera and photographs.
In one, he lifted his Leica and captured
my mother behind the window.
Today I feel the distance between them—
my father standing outside the house on Pavilion Lane,
my mother's hand parting the curtains,
her face veiled
by stitched flowers of delicate lace.

The Biscuit Tin

My father preferred Kodachrome slides to prints.
In the late fifties in Savannah
I remember him sitting in the dark
behind the projector, the beam of light
shooting across the room,
the white screen filling with image after image,
the sound of locks opening.
I piled pillows on the floor
and lay propped on my elbows, enraptured,
as if I were seeing into my father's mind.
I can't say what audience of ghosts
joined us in the dark
for my father's slide shows,
yet my father addressed them,
explaining where and when he took each photo
and offering elaborate backstories
to the picture of an ocean liner
docked at Southampton
or the family building sandcastles
on the French Riviera
or his DeSoto,
lost on winding roads in the Black Forest.
Over the years, my father held fewer
and fewer shows; eventually
he put away the projector and screen
and stored the slides in the attic
with the Christmas ornaments and old clothes.
After his retirement to the ocean cottage,
he kept them in metal boxes at the back of his closet,
keeping the film dry from the ocean air

and out of the strong light.
When I finally brought them home
to have prints made—
the Kodachrome slides must have been fifty years old—
I was stunned at their clarity and vivid color.
I made copies, the photos as pristine
as if they were taken only yesterday.
I mailed the photographs in an old English biscuit tin,
so my father could regard their intricacies,
each moment so fresh and delicate.
When I look at the photos, time collapses
into a darkened room pierced by a sword of light.

Help

My father found a tiny house in Eastcote. Mother
did not know how to cook,
so Mrs. Bucket, the housekeeper,
left father's supper on the stove
before catching the evening bus.
I never knew Mrs. Bucket,
though I've always pictured Mrs. Gamp
from Dickens's *Martin Chuzzlewit*.
The pages turned, Mrs. Bucket died,
and in summer I was born.
A German nurse, who to this day
must drift like a dark cloud over my first winter, was
hired to watch over me during the day. When our
mother and father went to a show or to one of the
many squadron parties,
the nurse stayed through the evening
and put me to bed. I keep pictures
in a biscuit tin of my parents and their friends—
laughing, diverted, their hearts gladdened
in English rooms with patterned wallpaper and
thick, heavy curtains.
In their fine and elegant tailored clothes
my parents look like movie stars.

A lifetime later, one evening over drinks,
my mother told a story about the German nurse.
A weekday afternoon. Already dark.
"I came home and the nurse—
I've long since banished her name—
fixed us tea." In the small living room,
the nurse confessed to my mother

that I had cried all day without rest
and would not stop crying,
even when the nurse shook me and shook me
to make me stop. My mother rose
in silence that afternoon
and opened the front door.
Her voice turned to iron—a voice I know.
"You need not return tomorrow."
I took a sip of my drink, then asked,
"Did you hire another nurse?
I know you were often sick those days."
I'd always thought we needed a nurse's help
because of my mother's vertigo,
which could cripple her at any moment.
"No, it wasn't anything like *that*,"
she corrected me with a smile.
I jiggled the ice in my glass
and waited for her to elaborate.
"The men of the squadron
were often away for days,
out of the country on flight missions.
So the American wives would gather
at the base club in the afternoon.
Smoking those strong English cigarettes
we'd talk about how different things were
from what we expected.
Then we'd set up four tables
and pass the hours playing bridge."

Scarlet Fever

Our family sailed from England when I was two.
We departed from Southampton
and crossed the Atlantic in a season of storms.
After seven sleepless days and nights of nausea
we landed in New York Harbor.
My father carried me in his arms
down the ship's gangplank.
For the next few months we lived
a peripatetic existence out of suitcases,
driving the DeSoto and staying with relatives.
Then—still with no home—
my father, the war pilot, reenlisted
and returned to duty in England.
He left us in Portsmouth, Virginia,
at his sister's tiny brick house
where I fell ill with scarlet fever.
The day I got sick,
my mother suffered a vertigo attack.
For days she could not lift her head
from the downstairs sofa, while I lay
feverish in a second-floor room under the eaves.
Fires inside me burned and raged.
The doctor snapped his black bag shut;
on the front door the health inspector posted
a quarantine sign:
no one was allowed
into or out of the house.
My sister and cousins whispered I'd be lost.
A telegram was sent to London.
An Episcopalian priest, I'm told,

knelt by my bed and prayed.
I cannot remember whose hand
held the cold compress
when my temperature spiked
and the end loomed near.
I still don't know
what hand gave me water,
my aunt's, my sister's,
or someone unknown to me,
or what angel to thank
for accompanying the child I was
through the valley of death.
And yet, after all these many years
and a long and lucky life,
whenever fever dreams wake me in the dark,
I sometimes feel on my brow that cool, damp cloth—
calming me, healing me—
one of a thousand mysteries I give thanks for
when I close my eyes at night.

Winston Churchill

It was many years before I realized
I had unconsciously modeled my cramped study—
the simple desk and narrow bed—
on Winston Churchill's office in the war rooms.
On the shelf I had *The World Crisis,*
which I would read and reread
for its thrilling and sculpted prose.
When I was young, Churchill was hailed
as an untarnished hero, and as a boy
I memorized lines from his speeches.
"We shall go on to the end," he'd said.
"We shall fight and never surrender."
Trembling in the dark, I'd lie on my childhood bed
and say those words aloud to the night,
and even now sometimes his gravelly English voice
floats through my dreams. Early on,
Churchill turned to painting as an antidote
to what he called the "black dog" of depression.
He painted hundreds of canvases
and his charming little book, *Painting as a Pastime,*
has always been a balm to me.
He painted the places he'd visit,
"an unceasing voyage of entrancing discovery"—
Venice, Mont Blanc, Avignon, Marrakech.
At his Chartwell country home
he'd capture the meadows and gardens,
the black swans on the lake.
They say Churchill enjoyed champagne,
scotch, martinis, and long conversations into the night.
Yet while others slept he labored

and wrote some fifty volumes of history and speeches.
After the War, my father bought a toby jug of Churchill.
Churchill is seated, holding his cane and gloves,
wearing his black hat and greatcoat,
the usual cigar between his lips.
After my father died, I asked my mother
whether I could have the toby jug she kept in the crystal cabinet.
She said no: it reminded her of life in England.
When Churchill was old,
he bid farewell to his ministers,
saying, "Man is spirit."
Today his portrait is darker,
his legacy more complex.
I think how dark my own portrait is
and wonder how clearly I see.
Some nights I picture that strange little boy I was,
lying in bed, vowing to fight to the death.
Then I remember that Churchill,
a man defined by war and empire, wrote
with exceptional beauty and lofty romanticism
in books such as *Amid These Storms*
that he would seek his little plot of redemption
and spend a considerable portion of his five million years
in a corner of heaven, painting.

Dickens's House

It was not until my sixties that I visited
48 Doughty Street. The London house—
its blue walls, the green velvet chair,
the simple dining table and walnut sideboard—
reminded me of Virginia and home.
I wandered the rooms, a child again,
feeling the old mix of love and sorrow.
When I climbed the stairs and stood
in the bedroom by the writer's bed,
I felt his absence. It then came to me
that the novelist's hard childhood—
the grief and humiliation—
was much like my father's.
Both had been sons of wealthy men
who lost their fortunes. Dickens's father
was confined in Marshalsea Prison,
and the child of twelve forced to work
in a boot-blacking factory to support the family.
There were no debtor's prisons in America,
but my father also sacrificed his youth
to toil and labor when the family lost everything.
Perhaps work—industry not for self but for others—
makes men good and wise?
After he became a father,
Dickens wrote *The Life of Our Lord*
solely for his children
and read it aloud to them every night.
He explained everything to his "beloveds"—
what locusts were and what a camel looked like.
A complicated man, Dickens taught them

that Jesus Christ is the kindest person who ever lived.
My father had few words and wrote no books,
yet even the way he would always open the door for me
was a kind of eloquence. Still,
I remember many times as a child
I wished he would have spoken.
Once, he found me in the garden, weeping.
Would life have been different if
he'd put a hand on my shoulder and quoted,
"The heavens will vanish like smoke.
Look to the rock from which you were hewn."

Church Bells

London is a city of churches
and my mother loved the church bells
calling to one another over the rooftops.
She said you could tell one church from another
by the sound of the bells,
the bells were that distinct, like human voices.
The bells at Saint Paul's overwhelmed her,
just as the grandeur of the sanctuary overwhelmed her—
she had always gone to a small and modest Carolina church
that had no bell at all.
My mother was a grown woman
before she fell in love with church bells,
but I was born to them. Riding in my pram,
the tintinnabulation of the English air
was a natural kind of music.
Even in America as a boy,
I knew the hour was late
not because the light had run out,
but because bells rang from the Methodist church.
Those Virginia bells weren't like England's consecrated bells
that pealed in rounds the liturgical hours
and tolled the deaths and births of kings and queens.
The Virginia bells weren't bells at all,
but a recording the Methodists broadcast
through crackling loudspeakers.
Hearing the not-real bells,
I knew it was suppertime
and that my mother was laying the table
and that the bells would ring for fifteen minutes
and I'd better hurry home, and I'd leave my friends

and walk through the autumn leaves in the dark.
Our house faced the church. My high attic window
framed the steeple and cross, silhouetted
against a purple sky and blowing clouds,
the haunted moon and lonely stars.
Even now, a lifetime later,
at the end of a winter day in Chicago
when I drive home in the dark to the suburbs,
my last turn is at a church with a gold dome,
where bells ring eventide over the rooftops
and I slow down to listen.

2

SHADOWS AND FLOWERS

Prophesy to the wind, to the wind only for only
The wind will listen.

T.S. ELIOT

Attics

I built a little makeshift room for myself
in our attic,
as if I, a lonely teenager,
were a poet hidden away,
starving in a Paris garret.
Attics are full of spiders and dust
and odd things
packed away in leather trunks,
but I felt warm and at home,
a thousand miles from anyone
who might know my name or care.
Nestled in among all the forgotten things
that one day would be thrown out and vanish forever,
I'd lie on the floor on my mattress, reading.
A tarnished lamp with a pull chain and tattered red shade
provided just enough light to dream by.
I had a boxed turntable
and I'd listen to Bob Dylan sing,
"It's all right, Ma,
it's life, and life only,"
then lift the needle and play the song again,
looking out a small, diamond-shaped window
that framed the black night.
My father kept belongings from the War
in military footlockers—
a gas mask, his leather flight jacket,
an ammo case, a revolver.
I remember finding a white cloth
with the Chinese flag
and Chinese writing painted on it

that my father said he was supposed to show his captors
if his plane were shot down and he lived.
There were foreign coins,
keys that opened lost locks,
medals still in their small blue cases
that spoke to acts of valor and bravery in war,
something I could never fully appreciate back then,
lying under the exposed rafters on my mattress
between antique bureaus and tall wardrobe boxes
with my father's old uniforms and my mother's wedding dress.

Vertigo

Of course I don't remember my mother
falling ill in the weeks after my birth
or recall who took care of me
and nursed me, but I do remember
how often during my childhood
my mother—confined to the sofa—
lay with the curtains drawn, perfectly still
and unmoving in the darkened room.
Vertigo was a word I learned early,
a word that contained mystery and power,
a word that could whirl the helpless world off its axis.
My job: to be quiet and not disturb Mother's rest.
Sometimes like a ghost, I'd sit across the room from her,
holding my breath and keeping vigil.
I felt concern and compassion and wished,
as hard as I could wish,
for her to recover and rise and be well.
Other times she'd ask to be alone
and I'd slip out of the house,
run off to the woods to wander and explore,
searching for a secret hiding place
or maybe just some flint arrowheads along the stream bank
that I could keep in my pockets to give me strength.
Sometimes I'd lie helpless beneath the trees,
as if I were dizzy and faint myself,
the branches of the loblolly pines
and the crowns of pin oaks spinning overhead.

Broom

One of the first jobs
I ever had
was sweeping in a warehouse.
I was handed a broom
and told
to make everything clean.
The warehouse—
vast as a cathedral—
was dark and dingier
than the rings of hell.
I peered,
but couldn't see to the end
of the filthy place
for all the shadows
and the mountains
of cardboard boxes.
Thick dust older than I
blanketed everything,
and the stacked boxes
formed a labyrinth
whose logic baffled—
it took me weeks to find my way
without getting confused or lost.
Forklifts burdened with boxes
groaned and lumbered,
changing any path
I thought I'd learned.
I remember
the blinding eye-shock
of sunlight

as loading-dock doors rose
to greet the delivery trucks.
Mostly I spent long days
alone with my broom
sweeping,
a task I performed
with great seriousness,
solemn in the gloom.
I was young,
and just wanted to do a good job,
the mean job
I'd been asked to do
and was paid for each Friday.
Looking back, I'm glad
I went into the grave of that warehouse,
and without ceremony,
as the days passed like a shadow,
was given a labor,
to keep things clean,
to pick up my broom and sweep.

The Blue Notebook

After spending a little time with eternity,
I stepped out of Sacré-Cœur
into the sunlight,
an old man on the basilica steps
with all the young people and their selfie sticks,
romantic couples taking portraits
as they fell into a pristine and hopeful love.
I looked down the hill
as if I were looking into the past
and grieved for time lost.
I remembered from earlier visits
that down the hill on Montmartre
there is a street named for Pierre de Ronsard,
the sixteenth-century Parisian "prince of poets."
A cultivar of rose was named after him
in remembrance of his sonnet comparing
fleeting beauty to a dying rose.
Yeats, in his book *The Rose,*
paraphrased Ronsard:
"And nodding by the fire, take down this book,
And slowly read." I remembered the first time
I heard those stories. I was a student
and rushed to the library to read the poems.
When I was young and poor,
traveling for the first time to Paris,
I sat on these same steps beneath the white basilica
and earnestly wrote in a blue notebook—
I always had a notebook when I was young—
that having no house or garden to call my own,
I would return home and plant roses in my father's garden.

I figured Virginia was a good place to grow roses,
even though I knew I would travel on
long before the roses bloomed.
I imagined seasons passing
and my elderly father—
his shears shining in the early sun—
carefully pruning the blossoming bushes,
grown generations old.
I envisioned a metal water-bucket brimming
with long-stemmed roses he would carry
with his unsteady gait back into the house.
I wanted him to arrange and leave the vibrant flowers
in a cut-glass vase to sparkle by the window
for my mother to discover. Even now
I see her smile shyly
as she pulls back her graying hair,
closes her eyes, and bowing, inhales the rich perfume.

Wordsworth's Barn

What dwelling shall receive me?

WORDSWORTH, "The Prelude"

In the Lake District I had no money,
no place to sleep, and no other option,
so I slipped past the poet's house
and broke into the barn behind Dove Cottage.
At dusk, when the tourist crowds had returned in buses
to their B and Bs in Grasmere,
I stole like a ghost through the gardens,
which were still and quiet
in the growing dark and chill.
I found the barn doors secured with a sagging chain,
but back then I was so skinny
that when I pried the doors apart
I easily slipped inside.
In the barn's obscure warmth, I stood listening.
Soon my eyes could make out shapes—
a wheelbarrow,
a work jacket hanging from a beam,
the silver grains of my own breath catching moonlight.
I fashioned a bed of fragrant hay,
wrapped my poncho around my shoulders,
lay my head on my knapsack, and slept.
Sometime in the night the snarling
of leashed Dobermans woke me.
The watchman blinded me with his torchlight.
"You mayn't sleep here," he said,
his accent strange and dreamlike to my sleepy ears:
Romanian? Finnish? "You mayn't sleep here,"

he called out again as I departed the cottage
through the whitewashed front gate.
Walking the road beside the lake Wordsworth immortalized—
the night crisp and clear, the lake full of light and shimmering—
I imagined the hills and crags watching
as I hiked the midnight miles to the deserted village.
A small brick station that sold tour bus tickets
was well lighted, but locked and empty.
Around back I found the men's room bolted,
but the handle to the ladies' room turned
and the door opened.
I spent the night on the concrete floor
of the single toilet stall,
more or less content with the arrangement.
I remember my last breath before falling asleep:
I drew air deep into my chest, held the breath,
then released the long, slow sigh I'd been holding back for years.

Tribulation

Years of tribulation did not open my eyes.
I lived in a farmhouse in the mountains
and tried to create a heaven of words.
I stood under stars with arms spread wide.

I lived in a farmhouse in the mountains.
I knew silent woods and clear streams.
I stood under stars with arms spread wide,
and prayed by the lake's black water.

I knew silent woods and clear streams.
I knew the moon. I knelt by the lake
and prayed by the lake's black water,
the weight of the past a heavy stone.

I knew the moon. I knelt by the lake.
I climbed crooked stairs to a desk,
the weight of the past a heavy stone.
I'd write all night, the lamp burning.

I climbed crooked stairs to a desk,
and tried to create a heaven of words.
I'd write all night, the lamp burning.
Years of tribulation did not open my eyes.

The Parable

Let both grow together...

Unable to sleep, the man opened a book
and nibbled the last of the day's baguette.
The first page he opened used the phrase
"clasping tares of domesticity." He recalled

the parable. The tares would be burned,
but the man wasn't exactly sure what a tare was.
The man knew the tare was Satan's weed—
the dictionary called it a "vetch"—

and his quick research revealed the grain
toxic to humans. And yet, during famine,
medieval monks shared a bread of vetch meal,
praising and giving thanks for its bitterness.

How to reconcile such humility
with the bitterness of life? The man
considered the end of the stale baguette,
hard as stone in his hand,

though early that bright morning
at the fragrant bakery,
he had purchased the baguette fresh,
still soft and moist and warm in its paper.

Lost

When I couldn't find the way,
I thought of Blackdog,
the blackest dog I'd ever seen,

so black that on a dark night
I couldn't see her
though I knew she was beside me.

That night,
I didn't know where I was,
and stood on the corner, lost,

remembering her brown eyes,
the muscular tail waving,
the joy that made her butt wiggle,

and the way she taught me
living is all about love,
and more—that one must

live fully in the moment,
like a dog, by instinct,
following one's nose,

pitiful, tenderhearted, humble.
Then I closed my eyes,
wanting the tug of the leash

in my hand, the *pull,* knowing
she was the clever one,
always deciding

where we should go,
days when we ventured forth
to walk in woods

or stroll through our small town.
Even in the battered blue car
when together we traveled everywhere,

I would turn
to her sitting beside me,
Blackdog looking straight ahead

and trusting the road,
staring through the windshield
as if only she really knew

where it was we were going,
as if even then she knew I was lost
but would help me find the way.

Omnia Omnibus Ubique

Back home the adults had said,
"In London you must see Harrods."
So I sacrificed a day I could have spent
wandering the National Portrait Gallery
and found my way to Knightsbridge.
I was twenty and could not have cared less
about department stores or shopping,
but from the outside Harrods was a palace of gold—
ornate facade, baroque-style dome,
and high windows like Versailles.
I confess I was impressed.
In the food hall, I didn't know
whether to admire the delectable cakes
or the art nouveau tiles of peacocks
drinking from the fountains of paradise.
I opened my guidebook
and for a few minutes lost myself in reading.
I read that not only the royals,
but many of my heroes
had shopped here—
Oscar Wilde and Sigmund Freud—
and that in 1921 A.A. Milne had bought
a Harrods bear for his son, Christopher Robin.
I wanted to purchase something small
yet elegant for my mother—
candlesticks perhaps—
but when I looked up from my guidebook,
there were no clerks in sight.
There was no one in Harrods at all.
I wandered the extravagant aisles alone until

a fireman in yellow helmet, turnout coat, and rubber boots
found me. He asked what I was doing.
"Nothing," I said, suddenly understanding with a chill.
This was the time of "the troubles,"
when the IRA had taken its bombing campaign to England.
When I innocently came out the front door—
emergency trucks everywhere,
red lights swirling,
the streets now completely cleared and barricaded—
a dozen somber agents and policemen turned, sharp and alert.
They looked me up and down, yet no one stopped me.
No one questioned me. The men were well trained.
In an instant they surmised who I was—
a harmless, lost, woolgathering Yank.

"Her Majesty"

Barely out of my teens,
I might as well have been climbing Mount Sinai
and hoping to see the burning bush
when I made my pilgrimage to Abbey Road—
that's how important the Beatles had been to me as a boy.
All through my childhood I wanted to go home to London,
where *they* lived and made their music.
The group's breakup was for me
the collapse of civilization,
the crushing of all hope.
The summer day I knocked on the door
of the white Georgian mansion,
a soft-spoken recording engineer greeted me
and improbably invited me inside.
He escorted the young man I was
down the hushed hall to Studio Two,
where I sat behind the idle console
with its myriad buttons, knobs, and sliders,
and gazed through the glass at the bare recording studio,
now silent and empty, haunted and ghostly,
the lonely microphones like three crosses
after the divine work was accomplished.
I wish I'd been *more* thankful
to be given so rare an opportunity,
so great a privilege,
but sitting before the console
all I knew was
Abbey Road marked the close of my childhood:
the Beatles were gone forever.
At the record's end,

I'd felt the black world spinning,
the scratch and hiss of nothingness.
I would have fallen into that abyss
if I'd not been saved by the sudden guitar,
the resurrected voice singing,
"Someday I'm gonna make her mine.
Oh yeah, someday I'm gonna make her mine,"
a line that will live forever
though it comes to a stop with a period,
and that last and final note.

The Camino

way, passage, journey, walk,

path, pilgrimage

We didn't go to London after all.
She was German
and we drove her old Citroën
from her father's home in Hanover
to the hills of the Alsace
where we stayed for a week in her uncle's cottage,
riding bikes through the countryside
and ambling through hamlets
decorated with red geraniums in window boxes.
From the Alsace we headed south,
following the winding Costa Brava
to Barcelona, then crossed the plain to Madrid.
If we'd parked the car
and walked the Camino north,
we might have done the pilgrimage properly,
but instead we drove to Toledo,
then on through forests to Lisbon and the sea
where we camped on Portugal's lonely beaches.
In Galicia we stopped at Santiago de Compostela—
as if "the field of stars" had been our destination all along.
We walked the town's cobblestone streets
and through colonnades crowded with university students.
In the great cathedral we wet our fingertips
in the seashell filled with holy water
while the blue smoke of incense
lifted up its fragrant prayers.
Neither of us knew how to kneel,
but when we touched the statue of Saint James

we wished for all the things we didn't know.
All I knew was that it was Spain and I was alive
and she beautiful, kind, and generous.
This was 1987, a time
that then seemed to move slowly,
yet whose fleetingness now astounds me.
Still, it is a sweet memory and cherished,
though I have not seen her for more than twenty years
and don't know where she is
or what wonderful things have happened to her.
We drove on to San Sebastián.
We pitched our tent on the edge of a vineyard.
At an old castle, at a table beneath the stars, we drank wine.
By candlelight we spoke in whispers
about all the things we would do with the lives we'd been given.

Typewriters

Years ago, I typed
on a manual typewriter,
a Corona. When the Corona died,
I bought a refurbished
Royal. Ideally,
a finished line rang
a small bell,
a sweetly signaled
new beginning,
and a silver handle
returned the carriage
to start a new line.
I'd type all day,
Blackdog under the desk
lying heavily on my feet
to keep me on task,
her brown eyes urging me on,
her dog-life a model
of fidelity and love.
It was almost as if
Blackdog were my muse,
telling me what to say,
translating from the keen
silence of a dog's mind
those intuitions and insights
I would never have dreamed
on my own. Unfortunately,
I proved to be a woeful typist,
always hitting the wrong keys
and sacrificing many white pages

for the sake of a single poem.
Under clumsy fingers
the type bars would
collide and jam,
the inspired moment stall
and die in a tangle of letters,
and soon I'd find
my hands blackened
from fiddling
with the ribbon and spools,
always starting over,
advancing a clean sheet,
and typing every line
over again slowly,
beginning with the title
while Blackdog snored
and dreamed of rabbits
and squirrels. The Royal
demanded virtuosity, vigor—
I had to strike hard
to trigger the keys—
but the daily work,
arduous and often unyielding,
nonetheless edified,
and typing on the Royal
purified thought
like a refiner's fire.
I'd read my poems aloud,
wise dog listening to verify
that her master understood
what he was saying
and offering finely tuned,
discriminating suggestions

as I revised draft after
sculpted draft in hopes
of permanence. Now
the world has moved forward—
words made of light.
But the old Royal
still sits on a bookshelf
and Blackdog lives in my heart,
so occasionally,
if only for the sake of nostalgia,
I'll roll a clean white sheet
into the faithful carriage
and type a few lines,
something Blackdog
would have me write—
a letter to my mother
or a silly note
I'll slip into my daughter's lunchbox.

Hallmark

Every year of high school
during the holiday season
from Thanksgiving to Christmas,
when the chill light was failing
and the days were growing dark,
my deaf mother and I worked
for minimum wage in the PX
of the naval base in Norfolk,
opening boxes and arranging
in the aisle's long display rack
dozens of colorful greeting cards.
My mother would turn to me
and read her favorites aloud
as if she were delivering
the greatest poem ever written.
I love my mother, and so I said
nothing. Instead, I'd grit my teeth
and steel myself not to hear
the sticky sentiment and clichés,
the expected, predictable logic,
the bland and lifeless certainty.
Those afternoons in early winter
were a budding poet's Freudian
nightmare, though looking back,
I've grown fond of the memory,
so much so that tonight I will sign
the card I've chosen, thanking her
for being who she is—my mother—
and send it off in a pink envelope.

The Hidden Meadow

The secret meadow lay between two hills,
with grass that rose up to a man's chest.
When I'd lie down, I'd disappear completely.
The grass would bend down gently under me.
The way a child makes an angel in the snow,
I made sorrow's shape. It was much like lying
in an open grave and looking up at heaven,
the clouds passing over, so far up and distant.
It seemed there was nothing else in the world,
just the tall grass bowing and bending, golden
in the sunlight, the meadow ready for the sickle,
every tall blade pointing upward, the distant
song of a few high white clouds in the pale sky
just enough to pull me through the sunny day.

The Used-Book Store

It seems like a million years ago
when I worked at the used-book store
in Los Angeles. Back then
there were bookstores everywhere,
each with its own personality.
The literary bookstore across the street from mine
sold little mimeographed magazines.
When you read the poems,
the blue ink would rub off the page
and stain your hands.
I loved that
and also that the poetry books
were prominently displayed
on old wooden shelves by the front door,
right next to the cash register
so you couldn't miss them.
The bookstore where I worked
specialized in medical books,
primarily psychiatric manuals,
but also hardbound tomes
of profound erudition,
often out of print and hard to find,
like Leonard and Virginia Woolf's Hogarth editions
of Sigmund Freud's monographs.
In the quiet bookstore
I'd dream of London and Bloomsbury
and Virginia hand-printing *The Waste Land*,
wondering what she'd make of my tattered
secondhand paperback copy
filled with a stranger's obscure

hieroglyphic marginalia.
Occasionally the front door's hanging bell would jingle
and wake me from my reveries,
sunlight spilling into the shop,
scattering the shadows
and making the dust sparkle
like a billion tiny snowflakes, drifting, weightless in the air.
And sometimes a crazy person would rush in—
a woman in a floor-length, flowered dress with long, wild scarves
or a man in a stained, rumpled suit.
They'd always pause by the entrance,
looking back through the glass door
to see whether they'd been followed
by government agents
or the Furies that plagued their waking dreams.
Then they'd see me.
They'd lean on the scarred old wooden counter,
and breathlessly ask all sorts of mad questions
as if I held the secret.
To these broken men and women
the bookstore was a place of refuge,
a kind of sanctuary or sacred spring;
but I was almost as lost and lonely as they were
and had no answer to life's riddles.
I was only twenty-two
and didn't know what to say
or how to answer
when the words they spoke
were like wisps from extinguished flames.
But sometimes
someone came through the door
who just wanted a particular title,
a hard-to-find book.

From behind the counter I'd say,
Yes, I can help you,
and the customer's eyes would brighten,
almost as if I had given him or her hope
or promised an explanation to the mystery
of why things are the way things are.
I knew exactly where
in the store the title was shelved
and I'd lead buyers
through a labyrinth of tall bookcases
and place the book into their hands like a prize,
like a palm leaf of victory
or a crown of triumph.
Those readers who sought rare books
and the street people with their mad questions
are all ghosts now,
haunting my dreams
or drifting like smoke through old memories
of long hours spent alone
in the dim and musky store
where I read Karl Marx or Sophocles,
while outside on the sunbaked boulevards
jacaranda trees lifted pale blue flowers to the sky.

The Leather Flask

Vintage glass flask
enclosed in warm brown leather
and crowned with a shiny
gold shot cap,

I bought you in Venice
from a full-moon-flooded shop
in a stormy gray autumn
when I was young, so young
the *acqua alta* and fog
almost made me believe
I could cross a tiny bridge
and disappear forever…

But I didn't disappear.
I carried you
next to my heart for years,
through bitter decades of life
before one summer morning
when the sun was shining
in the crowns of the maples,
I stepped into the garden,

unscrewed your cap,
and lifting my hand
in a wordless toast,
slowly poured you out.
The day hot, the sun high,
you were a fountain,
the golden whiskey sweetly
fragrant as it soaked into the earth.

After, I kept you in a drawer
beneath my softest sweater,
safe with the poems I still show to no one.
Then one of those wretched days came:
the sun dark, the moon broken.
I brought you forth again—
handsome leather flask from Venice!—
and carried your emptiness to my study
where I placed you, regal and royal,
on a gold stand on the bookshelf,
honored and remembered among the lucid tomes.

Now your emptiness stays with me always,
your leather armor
protecting a vessel of glass.
And the little gold cup from which I once drank
shines each time
I turn on my reading lamp,
reflecting the light and reminding me
how much I have yet to learn
about mystery and doom, peril and freedom.

Blue Plaques

In London Laura and I made a game
of searching alphabetically for blue plaques.
By St. James's Square Laura found
the residence of Lady Astor,
the first woman to sit in Parliament.
I found Elizabeth Barrett's house on Wimpole Street.
Had our children been with us,
we might have stayed with the rules
and kept playing, but when one sees
a blue plaque everywhere one looks
history overwhelms the imagination.
Laura said, "Think of it.
For hundreds of years
under the same London sky
people have been busy writing novels
or composing symphonies
or trying to change the world."
Dickens, Handel, Vladimir Lenin.
We bought a guide and turning the pages
we knew we'd never have time to find them all—
T.S. Eliot, Béla Bartók, Emile Zola.
It was almost a relief
to take the Underground out to Eastcote.
Walking Pavilion Way together,
we passed white picket fences
and front gardens crowded with flowers.
We surprised ourselves.
Between the two of us,
we knew all the names—
pansies, nasturtiums, roses, petunias,

daisies, snapdragons,
black-eyed Susan and sweet William.
Here among the anonymous row houses,
there were no blue plaques,
no commemorative inscriptions
to take us away from the moment,
husband and wife, strolling hand in hand, just quiet.

Rainstorm

A sudden silence and hush in the trees—
as if a shadow of veils came to walk
the garden path, a shadow made of bees
or all the erased words once made of chalk.

In the classroom, too, silence had fallen
over the students. And their wise teacher,
now speechless, his glasses off, seemed small in
contrast to the hard rain, heaven's preacher.

Rain falls without vain words to speak the truth:
all good things can be contained in the frame
of the heart. This we know. And while the azimuth
of a dead star can be measured and named,

a raindrop's crystal ball falls so fast
we cannot see to see that which will last.

Villiers Street

Today I walked in circles in Ruislip
looking for the old stone church
where sixty-one years ago I was baptized.
My sister had given perfectly good directions
and St. Martin's couldn't have been easier to find,
having stood in the same place for eight hundred years.
Over the door of the church an inscription:
"This is the House of God. This is the Gate of Heaven."
I lingered in the graveyard among the weathered stones,
the old names erased by time,
as if they'd all been written with water.
Yesterday at the Wallace Collection,
I discovered a painting that awed me
for its balance of clarity and mystery.
The painting seemed a perfect work of art—
the warm gold hues of the temple, the realistic figures
of the rabbi and priest reading scripture,
the Jews at a table studying the genealogy,
the kneeling Joseph and Mary off to the side,
and the holy infant, so very small,
yet now named and the source of light in the center
of that canvas painted by the artist
Christian Wilhelm Ernst Dietrich
in the 1700s. The catalogue said Dietrich
was internationally sought-after and successful,
though "today he is all but forgotten."
My father took with him all his untold stories
of love and war; my aged mother is forgetting
the life she's lived. The clouds clearing,
blowing away like nothing until nothing is left

but endless blue. Today
in the dimly lighted church
I tried to imagine my mother and father
holding me as an infant,
the scallop of water,
the water drops cool on my brow,
the prayers that were said. It seemed a vain exercise,
but then late tonight I was walking home
down Villiers Street under the old streetlamps.
On the sloping cobblestone lane
that runs down to the Thames, I saw a fox.
The fox trotted right up to me,
paused a long moment and looked me in the eyes
as if it had something to say.
Then the fox turned down a narrow passageway
and disappeared through an iron grate
by the Embankment Gardens where,
already in late winter,
the flowers have risen and are blooming.

English Lit

In twelfth grade our class read Milton,
Wordsworth, Samuel Pepys, Keats, and Shakespeare.
We reluctantly took turns reading aloud,
but besides that I don't think anyone ever said a word,
not even when Pepys described the plague
and London's doors marked with a red cross
and "Lord have mercy upon us" written there.
No, we all kept quiet and refused to let words
open the doors of our already diminished young hearts.
One winter day I came late to class,
slipped into the back of the room
and slammed my books hard on my desk.
"Poetry!" I screamed, "Poetry!
This world is tearing me apart—
there's blood coming from my eyes and ears!"
The students turned around in their desks
and watched as my feigned fury and outrage turned to tears,
my shoulders heaving, my face buried in the fists of my hands.
The teacher told the class to wait, took my arm,
and escorted me, shaking and unsteady, out of the room.
In the empty hallway she waited as I pulled myself together
then congratulated me on my performance.
When we returned to the room,
our normally demure teacher explained to the mystified students
that she had conspired with me.
She had asked that I come to class free and unbridled
and to give voice to my deepest feelings.
"*That's what poetry is,*" she told the class.
"It is for our sake," our teacher said,
"that the poet wails and laments at roseate dawn,

or howls triumphant paeans
into the midnight of despair.
Bear witness: like the stoical English,
we go through our days in deadening silence,
hollow men with faces like masks.
And like the staid, uncomplaining English,
we need our poets."

Brussels

My dream life takes me
to faraway places—
inside a painting by René Magritte,
or a ruined chapel
in the woods in Italy,
or that time in Brussels,
when I was twenty.
I remember
standing in the high-ceilinged apartment,
parting the lace curtains,
and furtively looking down to see
two men in dark suits and hats,
assassins who had followed me home,
standing openly
in the light of the streetlamp,
then hiding in shadows
by the park's stone wall.
I see myself at the tall casement window,
my thin hand testing the latch,
my worried eyes of clouds and sky,
my suitcase open on the bed behind me;
but then again
it's also true
that I can't remember
whether that day in Brussels
I was actually followed
or I dreamed the whole affair.
It no longer really seems to matter.
The assassins stalk and pursue me still,

biding their time outside my house in the dark,
whispering in French under the pines
and waiting for an opportune moment,
while upstairs in our bedroom, my wife
and I enshroud our faces in white cloth
and embrace the mystery of the other.

Here on Planet Earth

My cabin was a quirky retreat,
out of the way and secluded,
a quiet place where a man
could find haven and heal.
Woodstove. Well-water kitchen.
One room for playing guitar,
one with light for painting.
Sagging old bookshelves.
Sleeping loft. Writing desk.
This beautiful world broken,
the sky cracked in two,
everything in ruins save
the mountains, a watercolor
perfectly framed by the window.
Notebooks tried to find words
for the beauty seen in hills
and azure crests flowing north
in one abandoned brushstroke.
The problem was deep and great.
Gazing at those blue mountains
I would lose myself in questions.
I know my life is like morning fog—
here a little while and then gone—
but the vows I made then I've kept.
The rolling fields and secret path
I walked those many years ago
through autumn woods and snow
were more than a blessing. The path
made life sweet, and sweeter still
for the sake of my madness and sorrow.

The Flight to Madrid

Noli me tangere

This little blue rag
on my desk
is all that's left
of the blue shirt
I wore in Charlottesville
when as a student I haunted
the cramped and musty stacks,
looking for something,
reading and taking notes
in longhand at my carrel
until the library
closed at midnight.
I'd carry books
by the armload
home—
Pound and Yeats,
William Blake,
André Breton and Mallarmé—
pile the books high on the table,
light a cigarette,
sit and read by the window,
listening. I'd roll up
my blue sleeves
and write something about
the moon. With a pen
forever in my pocket—
ink stain over my heart like a badge—
and carrying in my book bag
Lorca's *Duende,*

I wore the shirt
all over tragic Spain,
where as a young man
I sat in a thousand cafés
and wasted summer days
sitting on park benches,
reading and thinking.
In the Prado I stood
before Correggio's masterpiece,
gazing at the risen Christ
and searching the sumptuous sky
glowing above the empty tomb.
If I could, this very night
I'd book a flight to Madrid
and hie again to that great city,
stroll the boulevards
and pass under the plane trees
that line and shade the Paseo.
I'd ascend the wide steps
to the museum I loved,
and there in the quiet galleries
I'd look again at the stone the angel rolled away
and Mary on her knees, swooning
in astonishment and wonder,
her yellow dress pooled around her
and turning gold in the light of dawn.
I'd look again at the Lord
lifting his hand and pointing to heaven,
showing the way,
dressed no longer in grave clothes
but a royal robe of deep blue,
the blue of my shirt,
the shirt I wore in Spain,

back when I found mystery everywhere—
in trains,
coffee shops,
the pages of every good book.
But like so many memories—
that spring in Torroella de Montgrí,
or standing by the stone seawall
in chilly San Sebastián—
the old shirt
is gone.
Like all the things of this world
that slip away with time,
it wore out,
the fabric unraveling over the seasons,
tearing at the elbows,
fraying at the cuffs.
I might have tossed the shirt out
but did not.
I finally took sharp scissors,
cut it up,
and used the pieces
to polish shoes
and silver trays.
I'd clean the windows
then wash the rag, fold it,
and use it again,
if only to clean my glasses.
The years have all come down to this—
a little blue remnant
saved on a desk,
a patch of blue sky
on which to lay a pen.

3

SECRETS AND KEYS

Before I compose a piece,
I walk around it several times,
accompanied by myself.

ERIK SATIE

The Bombed-out Library

All these years, this one photograph
has been with me, steadfast, a marvel
framed on my bookshelf:
an old black-and-white picture
of a bombed-out library in London.
The Luftwaffe had firebombed the city at night,
striking at its heart. Every building
had burned to the ground
or been bombed to rubble,
all but the old library, which stood inviolate.
It is the morning after the air raid
and from inside the library the English sky
is visible through the missing ceiling.
The roof's mortar and beams—
along with several book ladders
and broken reading tables—
lay mounded on the floor.
Amid the wreckage, three Englishmen
in long coats, suits, and bowlers,
calmly browse the bookshelves,
stepping on broken glass and scattered bricks
as if it were an ordinary day in London.
The books have not fallen from the tall shelves,
but somehow still stand neat in their rows
unperturbed, a wonder. English light
falls unbroken on the men's shoulders;
the spines of the books are bright;
the dust in the air is luminescent.
Each man finds a book,
takes it from the shelf, opens it, and reads.

Freud's Glasses

I had mixed feelings about visiting Freud's home
in Maresfield Gardens, a short walk
from Hampstead Heath and the Keats house.
I didn't want to stir up the old wretchedness,
yet when I stood in the doctor's office,
I felt no shame, no sin, only a sacred calm,
as if I'd come to a place of refuge and acceptance.
The famous round-rimmed glasses—
casually displayed on the desk
as if the doctor had just stepped away for a moment—
twinkled in the pallid window light.
I imagined putting the glasses on
and seeing myself when I was young
and trying to find a way through a series of breakdowns.
I recalled the first time I delivered myself
to the emergency room. I couldn't explain—
and the worried interns didn't know what to do with me.
I was taken to see the head of psychiatry,
a middle-aged woman who told me I
"shouldn't take life so seriously."
I went home and sat in the dark, wondering
what Sartre or Rothko might have said.
In the ensuing decades I wrote books
and went broke paying one doctor after the other.
Impossible task, staying alive,
yet my heart sought the light.
Had Freud stepped back into the office,
I'd have asked how to account for my late awakening
and is it all right with him that I use a word such as *heart*?
I opened the museum guest book,

signed my name with a flourish,
and drew a heart pierced by an arrow.
Then I bid farewell
to the totems and coffin masks and statues of Eros,
and walked through the quiet neighborhood
until I found a tea shop. Sitting by the window,
I wished those young interns from my past could join me.
I'd pour tea and we'd talk about everything—
suffering and poetry, futility and the fullness of life,
the privilege of being human,
the sun that rises from an ocean of sorrow,
the light that floods our world.

Rilke and Rodin

In Meudon is
Auguste Rodin's hilltop home,
and I'm sitting on the lawn in the warm sun,
doing a little work with my pen and notebook
at a green, wrought-iron, round table
much like the table I have back home.
I'm wondering what it was like to be sensitive young Rilke,
the great master's secretary,
watching the old sculptor with his chisel and mallet.
In their day, these hills were farms and vineyards.
Horse carts climbed the slopes to deliver stone,
and carriages brought customers to see the sculptures.
Rose and Camille vied for Rodin's attention,
his affection, but Rodin told Rilke,
Rien que travailler.
Work. That was the key.
Rilke envied Rodin's ability to rescue
inwardness from stone.
That inwardness
was what the poet wanted to achieve with words,
though he had yet to find a way.
Rodin told Rilke
that before he could ever hope to make a poem
he must first learn to see.
That was the secret. *Secrets and keys,*
I write in my notebook, then doodle some lines,
which become trees on the distant hills.
I draw an eye in the empty sky, then another eye,
then fill two pages with all-seeing eyes.
Du mußt dein Leben ändern.

The ancients believed thought and intellection
resided not in the head, the place of the crown,
but in the torso where we feel things,
the heart bright as the sun in its rib cage.
When a god looks at you with his true vision, Rilke said,
there is no place to hide.
Rilke believed, as I do now, in illumination,
the astonishment of transformation,
but the lost, dark young man who read Rilke's poems
believed *he* needed to change his life
every day, like a shirt.
Sitting at the green iron table
surrounded by the flowering forsythia,
I see Rodin's gardens are not unlike my own.
There is no view of Paris
or paths of crushed stone that ramble
down a terraced hillside through vineyards,
but still I miss my own Meudon,
my lawn and white birdhouses,
the sparrows and finches
that sing in my spruces and maples.
The sad fact that Rodin had no cherry trees
inspires a fondness
for the tender way my cherry trees
reach down and comfort me
as I dream at my table
while my children swing in the hammock
and light plays with time through the leaves.
This morning when I woke
in the dark of a tiny Paris apartment,
I couldn't have imagined
a place like the Villa des Brillants,
but now that I'm here,

writing in my notebook at a table on the lawn,
I see how familiar it all is, how much like home.
Looking at the artist's steeply gabled redbrick house
I half expect to see my wife open the high bedroom window
and in a flowing nightgown lean out—
her hair disheveled and wild—
calling down in French to ask
what I'm doing
and would I like to come upstairs.
She knows perfectly well I'm working,
that I've found the secret, the key,
but she also knows I'll close my notebook
and climb the stairs to join her.

"The Drunken Boat"

This morning on the rue Férou,
I found myself caught unawares
by Arthur Rimbaud's poem
carved on a wall that runs the length of the lane.
In the narrow cobblestone street
I translated the first lines into the air
then stepped aside
to let a bicycle rattle past.
The bicycle woke me to the fact
I was walking Saint-Germain's winding streets
a little bit like a drunken boat myself,
adrift on a sea of reveries.
Ahead I could see the spires of Saint-Sulpice
and over my shoulder the Luxembourg Gardens.
I walked the empty lane a few slow steps at a time,
gazing up at the poem,
deliberating.

When I was young
I carried Rimbaud's poems
like a talisman in my coat pocket,
finding in him a visionary comrade
and in the drunken boat's desire to be free
hope for my own future.
La vraie vie est absente, he said.
He thought the real, true life
was absent, that we aren't really
a part of this world. At nineteen,
Rimbaud gave up writing,
left France for the West Indies and Africa,
became a soldier, a deserter,

ran guns in Ethiopia, had his leg amputated
and died at forty, a penniless businessman.
His letters describe life without poetry or love:
desperate, wretched, preposterous, gloomy.
Hélas! que notre vie est donc misérable!
"Alas! That life should be so miserable!"

Toward the end of the lane,
on the other side of the wall above the poem,
cherry trees were coming into bloom,
pink and white branches reaching into the sky.
Perhaps because of the generous light
and the delicate blossoms
the poem's final image moved me—
a sad child at twilight
squatting by a cold black puddle
and releasing a toy boat
frêle comme un papillon de mai—
"as fragile as a May butterfly."
There at the wall
I had to finally acknowledge—
I must have repressed it when I was younger—
that Rimbaud the man was never free,
never happy or loved,
never content to be a little boat
bobbing about on a sun-drenched, windswept sea.
I tried to feel the poem as I did when I was a teenager,
tried to catch the fire that meant so much
when life seemed overwhelming
and I was breaking.
I remembered the photograph
I've kept on my desk over the years—

the boy's chaste white blouse, the angelic face.
I reached out and ran my hand over the wall's carved letters,
a wistful reminder of youth's bright hopes
and bottomless despair.

And now, sitting here
in my apartment at midnight
writing in my diary
and sipping wine
by a tall window opened to song and laughter,
I find myself describing the rue Férou,
Rimbaud the seer,
and the contrast of his reality.
Then I remember the moment
the bicycle and rider rattled past
over the bumpy cobblestones,
the Frenchman in his tweed jacket
half smiling,
his jaunty cap and sunglasses,
the books and bread in his basket bouncing.
"Maybe," I write, "I could be
like him, the man on the bike,
more or less content at the end of the day,"
and then I imagine
the rider lying on a sofa
in a small apartment and reading by lamplight,
a Paris moon in the window,
a bicycle leaning
by the door in the shadowed courtyard.

The Gift

Last night,
walking in the Latin Quarter
and dreamily following
the narrow cobblestone passageways
wherever they led
and losing myself in the crowds
carousing outside the brightly lighted bars
and hideaway restaurants,
I saw Man Ray in a gray suit
stepping through a doorway
and up narrow stairs. The lights
went on in a second-floor apartment,
and through the sheer white curtains
I could see he was conversing
with Kiki, his model and muse.
Kiki looked fabulous
with her big eyes
and straight black bangs.
She was the kind of spirit who would enchant
Man Ray's famous guests,
cook for them, woo them,
and at evening's end,
sing for them.
I thought to ring the bell
and tell Kiki
that Man Ray's photograph
of her naked back turned into a violin
is famous, that *Le Violon d'Ingres*
is now pictured on calendars
and even on the postcard

I dropped this morning
into the yellow mailbox.
I thought to tell Man Ray
that seeing his *Indestructible*
Object changed the way I looked
at everything, but then realized
words can't really explain why
I embrace such a mad thing—
a metronome with a cutout of an eye
glued to the pendulum.
Suddenly the lights went out in the apartment.
I had the feeling that Kiki and Man Ray
were looking down at me,
looking up at them.
Alone in the milling crowds
of the Latin Quarter at night,
I looked for words to tell Kiki and Man Ray.
Then, as if he could hear me,
Man Ray opened the window
and leaned out.
His pomaded hair shone in the street light—
I could see the rakes of his comb.
A purple stain, perhaps of wine, bloomed on his lapel.
He asked me why I didn't ring the bell and told me
Erik Satie was with him the day he created
his first readymade—the flatiron with nails.
I told him I love the flatiron with nails.
He said it was a century ago
and he didn't speak French
and Satie didn't speak English,
but that Satie said *ce n'est pas important.*
They had been drinking hot grog—
it was winter in Paris and cold—

and they were walking to Man Ray's gallery show
and saw the iron in a shop window.
Man Ray bought the iron then and there
and with Satie searched for glue and nails.
Then Kiki too leaned out into the light,
her black bangs falling forward, her face pale, her eyes
glistening, her neck long and white against the dark room.
"He called it *Le Cadeau*"—her musical accent was charming!—
"which in English means 'the gift.'"
"I know, I know," I said, wanting to say more,
wanting to say I've known *The Gift* all my life.
Kiki asked did I know Man Ray grew up
among sewing machines and flatirons—
his father a tailor, his mother a seamstress?
I told her that's interesting. I didn't know that.
I told her my grandfather was a blacksmith.
"He made wheels, gates, and tools. I think
he actually made flatirons, too," I said.
"A godlike man who dared seize the fire,"
Man Ray said. "Yes," I said, "that's right."
I explained that my grandfather died
before I was born. My mother
was with him when his heart stopped.
"*Je suis désolé,*" Kiki said. "*Je suis désolé.*"
In the upstairs open window
behind the white curtains
the two of them became
darkening shadows.
Kiki and Man Ray.
Muse and artist.
Later,
walking home at midnight
on the cobblestone quais along the Seine

and looking down into the black water
and the golden lights reflected there,
I regretted that I never knew my grandfather,
never got to talk with him at his work,
the ring of the anvil, the heat of the forge.
Then I heard Kiki's voice
speaking to me as clearly as if she
and Man Ray were walking beside me.
"It doesn't matter," she said.
"It doesn't matter that you never talked.
The forge is a gift. Indestructible.
Like stories about your grandfather
and his little girl in the house practicing piano,
keeping time with the all-seeing metronome."

I Call My Mother Once a Week

My mother lives in a land
of disaster and tragedy.
Yesterday on the phone
she said, *Look, a small
white plane just crashed
in the yard.* Good thing
it didn't land on the house
I said, not knowing what to say.
It was like the time she'd said,
*A house down the street burned
to the ground,* and I'd said,
You're kidding, and she said,
It was an inferno, then asked,
because I know about words,
whether she had used the right one.
I said *inferno* was exactly right,
and she added that it was night,
pitch-black, and the young
family of four had died in the fire.
They couldn't be saved? I said.
They couldn't be found, she said,
and in the silence on the phone
we could almost hear the flames.
To change the subject, I inquired
about her crazy friend, Nancy.
Nancy was always up to something.
Arrested for murder, my mother said.
What? I said. *She hired a hit man
to kill the wife of the man she wants
to marry. Tragedy is, the man*

didn't even really know Nancy.
Of course there's nothing to say
in response to a story like that,
so I just said, Sounds like true love,
and my mother said, *It does, doesn't it?*

At the Carnavalet and the Cognacq-Jay

I show my late father Voltaire's writing chair—
comfortable, not too big or soft,
resting on curved legs with tiny wheels
and brilliantly rigged with two
pivoting mechanical iron arms,
one holding a reading panel
for manuscripts, the other
a desk with drawers for ink and pens.
I could live in that chair
for the rest of my life,
I tell my father,
then show him Proust's room—
the cork-lined walls,
the tiny bed of dreams,
the drop-leaf rosewood writing desk
where the novelist built
a "cathedral of words."
I point out the lamp with its green shade,
the hardback notebooks
on the nightstand.
I tell him Proust's handwriting
was nearly as bad as mine,
and he says
that's because writing flows like rapids,
not like something printed or typed.
My father invites me to look at Napoleon's
mahogany campaign box
with its "necessaries"—
crystal glasses, silver razor,
ebony vials of cologne,

gold mirror, ivory snuffbox.
Fancier, he says,
than what he was used to,
back when he was a soldier in battle.
I look at his eyes, so blue.
When I was growing up in Virginia,
he regaled me
with a thousand war stories,
more about comrades and travel,
than dying and battle
—stories I still remember verbatim today.
My father let his life bear witness—
the courtesy of his tested heart,
the tears and kindness.
If only in that, I pray we are the same.
As we descend the winding staircase
beneath the Carnavalet's chandeliers
he asks am I hungry.
We walk two blocks
to a little bistro for lunch.
We've already eaten there three times this week
and from the menu today,
we ask for escargots,
rabbit leg, steak tartare,
lamb with herbs, duck confit
—unlike the soup he typically ordered,
so harsh were his lessons from the Depression.
We devour huge bowls of chocolate mousse
and over coffee
he asks about my sabbatical, do I miss my family.
I love Paris,
but it's hard being so far from Laura.
And I miss the children—

their laughter and wisdom.
He says he felt the same,
all those air-force years he was away,
flying around the world,
his military life so far from us.
We touch our glasses
of eaux-de-vie—
I'm drinking plum, he's sipping pear—
and smile at the paradoxical truth:
even now, knowing what we know,
neither of us wants to leave the Marais
and go home. After lunch we walk
down rue Elzévir to the Cognacq-Jay,
where my father grows rhapsodic
over the Canaletto paintings of the Grand Canal.
My father's been everywhere,
but never to Venice, city of dreams.
In his honeyed southern voice
he tells me Venice looks very different
from where he lives now.
I tell him maybe we could
book an overnight train
and go there.
We could sleep
in the narrow bunks,
like soldiers in army cots.
His posture changes.
"Maybe," he says.
He leans closer to the Canaletto and the canal,
almost touching the canvas with his nose
to see the master's brushstrokes,
light on water
and royal palaces,

the black gondolas,
sky,
and majestic clouds.
My father and I
didn't talk like this when
we were younger and he was alive—
we were too different;
but now we talk all the time,
and understand each other perfectly.

Pont des Arts

> The pain passes,
> > but the beauty remains.
>
> RENOIR

Wandering the Musée de l'Orangerie with my sister,
we find a bouquet of roses painted in 1878 by Auguste Renoir,
voluptuous white roses placed on a red velvet chair.
My sister says Renoir's last word was "flowers"
and that toward the end of his life he said of painting,
"I think I am beginning to understand something about it."
His quest for beauty was relentless, tireless,
though when painting flowers, she says
his mind was always calm, restful, and full of good cheer.
I imagine his final year—the brushes lashed to his wrists,
the wheelchair and the makeshift sedan with bamboo poles
on which he was lifted and carried through the Louvre
so he could see the hallowed galleries one last time.
Bouquet dans une loge—so beautiful, I rub my eyes.

*

Sitting in the sun on the steps of the Palais Garnier,
my sister holds out her cellphone to show me a Degas—
the light gracing a girl, a ballerina in a yellow tutu.
She says the ballet originated with men in the royal courts,
courtiers who executed deep, elegant bows to the king,
and that young women like Degas's little girls
(who always remind me of my golden-haired daughter)
did not perform until the time of the Revolution
when the ballet at last became a revelation
of what the body is born and made for—

a dance that moves to the music of time.
"Which," my sister says, leaning back on the opera's
warm stone steps to get the sun on her face,
"*is* the golden light—the yellow light in the Degas painting."

*

The day is filled with light, so like two pilgrims
we walk to the Seine and linger on Pont des Arts,
the bridge where ten thousand gold and silver locks
inscribed with names and fastened to the grillwork
flash and gleam, symbols of undying love;
below, the emerald water is swiftly flowing.
For a moment in time among the love locks,
the two of us lean against the black rail,
poised between heaven and earth.
Locks and wishes. Perhaps the river
makes my sister think about her son.
I find myself pondering locks
that have been broken, discarded,
divorce and death, the faded memories.

*

Outside the Church of Saint Eustache,
the *Écoute* sculpture—the giant head
with the hand cupped to its ear, listening—
hears our footsteps and knows we're coming,
but because its eyes are closed it doesn't see us
when we take its portrait with our cameras.
The church's massive wooden doors swing open
and in a dark niche, a bright triptych by Keith Haring
proclaims the Lord's birth, life, and death,
the story etched into a panel of gold.

Compared to its impressive baroque neighbor,
Peter Paul Rubens's *The Pilgrims of Emmaus*,
the Haring is so simply drawn it seems, my sister says,
created by the hand of a child, innocent and full of faith.

*

In Saint-Paul-Saint-Louis my sister talks about her son,
the way his golden hair would fall straight down
when he hung upside down in his tire swing,
a silly smile crinkling his eyes. She relives
the day her five-year-old drowned in the river,
the river behind her house that still flows each day,
as timeless as the Seine. Each day in this church,
we find ourselves drawn to the blue prayer candles
lighted by those who came before us and still flickering.
Our fingertips touch the holy water in the pilgrim's shell.
Love and loss are something my sister knows about,
the way Renoir knew a little something about beauty.
She says pain and grief are omnipresent,
yet somehow love and loss have been spun into gold.

*

Open-eyed in the dark on the sleep-sofa, I consider
knocking on the bedroom door and waking my sister
to ask whether she thinks we'll see Renoir's roses in heaven—
a silly question that worries me and keeps me awake.
Next morning I'm still drowsing when her key rattles
the antique lock, opens the door, and the early chill
lingering on her coat is carried into the apartment.
The sweet aroma of fresh baguettes from Miss Manon's
stirs my imagination and the burbling coffeemaker
opens my eyes and calls me to new adventures.

On the kitchen table a tin pot of roses from the Bastille,
the powder on the petals calm and full of good cheer
and "with whose sweet smell," my sister says, quoting Shakespeare,
"the air shall be perfumed—"

Water Lilies, Green Reflections

I'm sitting before Monet's *Nymphéas: Reflets vert.*
The tiniest brushstroke of viridian green pigment
textures the water like shot silk.
A woman in a blue kimono
with a black obi knotted at her back
glides dreamlike through the Orangerie.
When she sits next to me on the bench
beneath the gauze-covered oval skylight,
I think of Ryōkan's poem—

>*Oh that my monk's robe*
>*were wide enough*
>*to gather up all the suffering people*
>*in this floating world—*

a poem I think Monet would have liked,
maybe even would have whispered under his breath
when he rose before blue-black dawn
and carried easel, canvas, and paint box
through the dark to his lily pond.
And now—
her embroidered silk sleeve alongside my old tweed coat—
drooping willow branches calm the purple water.
The green of the lilies deepens.
The shadows darken.
I'd like to ask Ryōkan
what brought the woman here this moment
that together we might imagine the bright clouds and breezes
blowing through the garden at Giverny.
Then I remember another poem the monk wrote
with his brush on a paper kite:

>*heaven-up-great-wind.*

Faith

I step onto the old, gray, wooden pier
that stretches beyond the sandy shallows

to the channel in the James, even though
halfway to the deeps

the barnacle-encrusted pilings,
buckled by time and tides, sink,

and the planks dive beneath clouds and sky
bright in the river;
        but if I keep walking the pier,

following the planks that now appear
suddenly close just below

the lens of the clear surface,
someone standing back on the shore

in their boat shoes would think
I'm walking on water.

Ravenous

At dusk I carry
a brown ceramic bowl
of drowsy bees—
the last bees on earth,
wings shimmering—
through the town square,
down narrow streets
to an empty house,
where I somehow open
the door with my elbow,
and once inside
shrug off my coat,
holding the bowl
first in one hand
then the other,
before climbing stairs
to a whitewashed room
with a wooden chair
and table where
at the stroke of midnight
I stand by an iron bed,
place the murmuring bowl
of drowsy bees
on a soft down pillow,
and with freed hands
light two tall candles.
Then at the spartan table
I sit all night
with pen and paper,
writing a book called *Honey.*

I write a line,
"the bitter is sweet,"
as one by one
the bees swoon,
lift from the bowl,
take murmuring flight,
and as if delighting
in a garden of flowers,
compass and buzz about my head.

The Sky

It's not much of an airfield,
just two grass landing strips
that crisscross
a few acres of pasture
as quiet as a country cemetery.
But when I go there and wait
for my deceased father,
before long he lands his plane,
a little white Cessna,
a two-seater he calls *Bird*.
He checks the controls
while I put on my headset—
we've done this many times
so I know the routine—
and when the tower says
we're cleared for takeoff
he gives it the throttle
and we speed down a runway
lined with bluegrass and clover.
Just seeing the clover rushing by
makes a difference,
and when the wheels lift
and *Bird* starts to climb, I feel
a sudden willingness to let everything go,
the terrible need to talk
or the compulsion to carry
all these stones in my heart.
From high in the air, the world below
looks small, which it is, and people

are so tiny they disappear.
Flying with my departed father
I find it very difficult to hold on to troubles,
and suddenly it is right to love everyone
as we burst free from clouds
and fly into the light.

Afterward

Leaving work late one summer night,
I looked up to the atrium—
drenching rain
polishing the skylight,
a darkly gleaming sheen on the glass
illumined every few moments
by lightning strikes
and rattled by concussive thunder.
I'd spent the day tinkering the line
"impossible task, staying alive,"
thinking about the rack and ruin of my youth
and what Hemingway had said—
"The world breaks everyone
and afterward
many are strong at the broken places"—
and then the storm's intensity
seemed to complete the day's meditation.
I dawdled in the doorway,
relishing the downpour,
smiling, twirling my umbrella,
a song gathering in my chest
as I studied the tempest—the wild sky,
the wind and rain, the flashing clouds,
torrents shining in the streetlamp's light.
I stepped out under the sycamores.
Walking the empty street,
instantly soaked and perfectly happy,
I began to hum a little tune.
The blowing rain felt good,
cool and refreshing,

and I was glad my hands carried nothing,
only a companionable red umbrella,
no books, no briefcase,
no burden to weigh me down,
my spirit so light I thought the storm
would lift me up and carry me away.
It almost made me sad to see my car
waiting that night all alone in the sea
of the flooded parking lot, the fierce rain
coming down so hard the shining asphalt
was blacker under its inch of water.
In the same moment, sudden lightning—
my eye just quick enough to see the swift spark
splinter and lash across the rooftops,
a charged finger that instantly sought the
tip of my umbrella, arced down the spoke,
then leaped to trace the curve of my right ear,
an almost amorous caress, thrilling
and tender as a whisper of longing
while darkness raves and rants and rails.
And that was all. In the empty
parking lot, keys in hand, I stood,
broken still perhaps, but italicized
and stronger than I'd been minutes earlier,
walking devil-may-care under the sycamores
and singing a little tune.

Nocturne

At day's tired end
when the children
have gone to bed,
Laura lifts the wing
of the grand piano
to its fullest glory,
sits at the keyboard,
and fills the house
with Satie, the melody
a serene flowering
so quietly intense,
so lucidly palpable
the children in their beds
hold their breath,
eyes shining in the dark
before they doze
and drift into sleep,
while in the stillness
of a shadowed and
lamp-lighted study,
their bookish father
sits at his old desk, listening.

The Manifestation

The night of the Perseid shower,
thick fog descended
but I would not be denied.
I had put the children to bed,
knelt with them,
and later
in the quiet kitchen
as tall red candles
burned on the table between us,
I'd listened to my wife's sweet imprecations,
her entreaties that I see a physician.
But at the peak hour—
after she had gone to bed,
and neighboring houses
stood solemn and dark—
I felt no human obligation
and went without hope into the yard.
In the white mist
beneath the soaked and dripping trees,
I lifted my eyes
into a blind nothingness of sky
and shivered in a white robe.
I couldn't see the outline
of the neighbor's willows,
much less the host of streaking meteorites
no bigger than grains of sand
blazing across the sky.
I questioned the mind, my troubled thinking,
and chided myself to go in,
but looking up,

I thought of the earth
on which I stood,
my own
scanty plot of ground,
and as the lights passed unseen
I imagined glory beyond all measure.
Then I turned to the lights in the windows—
the children's night-lights,
and my wife's reading lamp—still burning.

Blue Stars

Yesterday I made a to-do list,
a dozen tasks I would undertake
and check off the list one by one.
But what did I do with my list?
Did I put it on the piano?
Did I set it down by the coffeepot?
I remember this morning
in my robe at the back door
contemplating frost icing the grass
and seeing a dark-eyed junco at the bird feeder.
How did I know it was a junco
and not a sparrow?
Maybe juncos and sparrows are cousins.
I thought about birds in nests
of twigs, reeds, briars, and straw.
The clear, cold sky brought to mind
the image of my late father, high up
and far away, flying
once again in his silver plane,
and I closed my eyes to admire
the many blue paintings
hanging in the gallery of my childhood heart.
Perhaps at that moment
I had the to-do list in my hand
and during my azure reverie
the paper slipped from my fingers.
I only know that when I opened my eyes
I saw it would be wise
to give my blue paintings away—
only then would my heart be free

to help those in need.
I resolved to put that on my to-do list,
and that's when I noticed
my to-do list had vanished.
Now the frost has died,
the sun is pushing noon,
and I'm still in my robe
with eternity hovering in the balance.
But no day is without its victory.
Because it is hiding,
I'll search for the lost little piece of paper,
and when I find it
I'll write down my heart's resolution.
Then I'll dress for the day and go out into the world.
With pen and to-do list in my hands,
I'll draw little blue stars
beside all the accomplished tasks—
buying milk,
picking up the laundry,
driving to the library,
and paying the fines for my overdue books.

After the Rain

I hurry through the early evening
down rain-washed Chicago streets,
carrying a great bouquet of flowers
upside down so the heavy weight
of so many red and yellow blooms
will not break or bend the tall stems.
The flowers are wrapped in white
paper on which a small envelope
has been taped. The aproned girl
in the florist's shop waited, while
pen in hand I looked into eternity,
wanting to write something equal
to the flowers' beauty, to her beauty,
then wrote my wife's name, *Laura*.

Andrew and William

Beneath pines blue in first light,
they washed in the cold stream.
Then the brothers broke camp and
leaned into the slope, ignoring blisters
and hands raw from climbing chutes
of jagged rock that bleached in the sun
at noon. In the shade of a stone outcrop,
they rested, saying nothing, then
determinedly chased their shadows
up the mountain until—the summit.
They gazed at how far they'd come
and out to the distant peaks at sunset.
They came down radiant with wonder.
What inspired them in that last light?

4

HOME

Would you prefer all those castles in Spain?
Or a view of the street from your windowpane?

VAN MORRISON

Prodigal

My aged father and I enjoy the silence between us
as we sit in our Adirondacks, watching the children
playing tag on the lawn and running in circles,
happy to be it or not to be it, happy just to be,
though I know they give no thought to being.
My father leans toward me ever so slightly
and out of nowhere tells me he should have died
at seventeen, on a sunny Sunday, a beautiful day,
much like today. On a lonely country road,
he was driving his father's new convertible—
he'd taken the car without permission—
and the car suddenly spun and rolled three times,
slamming against a pole and sailing into a summer-
stagnant ditch. My father had no idea how or why—
the road spinning like a needle in a crazy compass—
but afterward, he said, there came an abrupt peace,
a long silence; then from pines and crowns of trees:
birdsong. A caravan of open-air cars slowly
driving from church to go picnicking at the beach
stopped when they saw my father by the road,
staring down at the half-sunken wreckage.
When asked if anyone had died, my father
met their gaze and told them he had no idea,
and in his muddy shoes began the walk home.
That seemed to be the end of the story. The children—
inexhaustible, exuberant—were now tumbling
and rolling in the grass, the sun a pinwheel in the sky.
The silence was green and blue and filled with light.
In his chair my father studied his grandchildren.
In time he lifted a crooked finger and added

that he walked the miles home and confessed
to his father, who refused to admonish him,
and after that day never gave the car another thought.
But the birds in the trees had brought it all back,
the disobedience and forgiveness. Then in the silence,
I looked up at the pines and heard the birdsong, too.

The History of the Desk

I like thinking about the history of the desk,
how once upon a time the desk
was nothing more than a tablet
on which to rest a quill and parchment.
That was long ago, when writing
was reserved for kneeling scribes
or the king's amanuensis,
though it is still inspiring to imagine
the sharpened quills and inkwells,
the long scrolls rolling off the tablet's edge
onto the floor. In the third century
Saint Augustine examined his heart with his pen.
His *Confessions* was the first modern book—
a self-examination—
but we will never know
what the saint's desk looked like.
In high school I had a desk with a sloping top,
like those of monks in ancient monasteries.
Late at night with candles burning
I filled notebooks with calligraphy, drawings,
my first poems. Recently in a Paris museum,
I saw Renaissance desks with secret drawers,
and once in a wealthy home
I touched a desk inlaid with silver and precious stones.
But the desk I have most loved in this life
is the nineteenth-century desk
my father found in a secondhand shop in London,
a simple writing desk with a walnut and leather top,
brass fittings, and spiral-turned legs.
Back then, after the War,

people in London were living on rations.
My father had no money either,
so he and the shopkeeper shook hands
and traded the desk for a bottle of American bourbon.
The desk came home with us from England.
As I was growing up, I'd stand before the desk
and imagine all the books that could be written
on that altar of leather and walnut.

The Egg

Will I ever shape a poem or work of art
more mysterious than the egg—
the pure white of the shell?—
the simple oval shape?—
the inscrutable world inside?
Heavy in the palm,
an egg's weight delights the hand.
A hundred years ago
my grandfather, a blacksmith,
sold eggs as a side business.
He raised chickens in three henhouses.
Because I once asked,
my mother wrote a little essay for me
called "Chickens." She wrote of how
she'd ride in the truck with my grandfather
to the train station. The Southern Line
brought wooden crates packed with chicks—
thousands of tiny biddies. She wrote
about going into the dark of the henhouses
to collect the eggs, sorting them by size—
small, medium, and large—
and placing them in baskets to sell.
Eggs helped the family survive the Depression.
The world was changing
and the blacksmith's days were numbered,
but my grandfather would not be defeated.
He worked at his forge until the day he died.
My mother wrote these memories for me
with blue ink in longhand
when she was almost ninety,

her cursive script flowing across the white page,
elegant and lovely, like rolling waves of time.
Maybe I inherited my love of mystery
from my mother, and the fire and iron—
the strength and resolve to stay at it—from my grandfather.

Hearts

I love English names, such as Richard the Lionheart
or Percy Bysshe Shelley. Richard's heart,
embalmed with frankincense, is buried at Rouen Cathedral;
and Shelley's ashes from the pyre
that burned on the beach near Viareggio
are buried in the Protestant Cemetery in Rome.
Oscar Wilde, penniless and alone,
died brokenhearted in Paris and lies in Père Lachaise.
Shakespeare is found in the town he was born in,
though he lived his life in London
where the Great Plague killed his sisters, brother, and son.
The Black Death shut down the theaters.
London's unholy darkness—
the filthy streets, the diseased Thames—
lit candles in the playwright's heart,
and Shakespeare wrote his sonnets.
I imagine the quill in his hand as he penned,
"to love that well, which thou must leave ere long."
No one knows the dark lady who inspired his verse—
how she lived or how she died.
The Great Plague killed rich and poor alike,
their love buried by the thousands
in church parishes and plague pits.
"Out, out, brief candle!"
Shakespeare knew: no one remembers
the names of the dead.

The Tantalus

My mother never had a drink
until she married at twenty-three

and visited her in-laws. When
the family ritually gathered at dusk,

my father's father took her arm
and revealed the secret

in his honeyed Tidewater lilt
that sounded like West Country English,

saying, "this is how it's done,"
as he graciously poured my mother

a single ounce of bourbon,
filled the glass with ample water and ice,

and instructed her to take all evening
to sip her drink.

For the next sixty-three years,
that is what my mother grew to love,

a tradition they called "toddy time"—
my mother and father each day at five

enjoying their sips of Virginia Gentleman,
lifting heavy Waterford glasses—wedding gifts—

that caught the light and sparkled.
I remember my parents

displayed their bourbon
in my grandfather's tantalus,

a locked oak liquor caddy
that held three square crystal decanters

with engraved sterling bottle tags.
The tantalus graced the hand-carved

English walnut and leather desk
with twist-turn legs

my father had found
after the War in a London shop

and had traded for
with a bottle of American whiskey.

That was long ago,
in 1953,

the year I was born.
The year my mother turned eighty-six—

the year of my father's death—
she stopped drinking.

She set her glass in the cupboard.
The tantalus and trinity of bottles

wait on the old desk
where she sits alone, penning

in her Victorian hand
long letters to her son,

telling him to live a sober
and quiet life, to mind

and watch over his family
and their rituals and traditions,

and on some still night
to find a moment to write her back,

which I do, now that I am older.

Walking Miracle

Today my mother is ninety-two
and we are sitting together in the sunroom
in the cottage that looks out over the bay.
We are talking about when I was three,
the year she was diagnosed with cancer.
The doctors told her she would die
and to set her house in order.
I was taken to live with my aunt and uncle
in Raleigh. Back then
adults didn't explain to children
things such as death and dying,
and I had never heard the word *abandoned*
or *orphan*. My uncle B.I.—
his name was Boyd Irwin—
looked like the Tin Man from *The Wizard of Oz;*
Aunt Ruby, old and beautiful,
could have been Glinda's mother,
a Good Witch. In the kitchen
Ruby would lift me on her knee
and ask did I have any sugar,
then snuggle and kiss me,
telling me I was sweet, so sweet.
Her lipstick left red marks—
beautiful wounds on my face.
The small house stood on a hill.
A horse-drawn ice cart climbed the road.
The iceman would open the door to the icebox
and gusts of mist would fly out
like ghosts into the summer air.
Aunt Ruby would buy a block of ice,

which the iceman lifted with leather gloves and tongs.
The ice was her gift to me.
I'd sit on the lawn by the flower beds in the hot sun,
watching the ice melt. The earth turned
and months passed and my mother didn't die.
The surgeries a success, she survived.
The doctors proclaimed her "a walking miracle."
When I recall the arc of my life,
my mother helps me remember
her sister Ruby's scent of powdered lilac
and how tightly Ruby held me when she kissed my cheek.
My mother says, yes, it was a long summer
the year of her illness.
She tells her stories simply, as a matter of fact,
then in the clear lens of the September light
she puts her warm hand on my arm,
reminding me with a knowing smile,
"We all need radical surgeries
and miracles to survive."

Bread Street

John Donne's life was a parable and a paradox.
Born on Bread Street, he was a Catholic
and a Protestant, a soldier and a priest,
a lover of women and a faithful husband.
At the end of his life the poet became
Dean of St. Paul's. His most famous line—
"never send to know for whom the bell tolls"—
is not from a poem
but from one of his devotions.
In St. Paul's there is a statue:
John Donne in his death shroud
rising on the Day of Judgment.
Some biographers say the poet's life
was a contradictory performance,
but I love the contradictions and complexity,
and see in him a seamless whole.
And yet I suffer. For years
I've taught his poems, hoping their fire
would burn and burnish my heart.
Whenever a student is brave enough
to say he or she doesn't understand
"Batter My Heart, Three Person'd God,"
I ask everyone to simply count the verbs—
batter, knock, breathe, shine, seek, rise,
stand, o'erthrow, bend, break, blow, burn,
make, labor, admit, defend, love, divorce,
untie, take, imprison, enthrall, ravish.
"That's a lot of verbs for a fourteen-line poem,"
I tell the class, hoping the verbs alone
will illumine and enlighten

that this is a prayer for the soul's sake,
and not a poem alone.
I read the last lines again:
"Take me to you, imprison me, for I
Except you enthrall me, never shall be free,
Nor ever chaste, except you ravish me."

The Philosophers' Banquet: A Cento Sonnet

> And what about salt?
>
> RICHARD JONES

Salt! Who comprehends her? —*Beethoven*

Salt is the daughter of freedom. —*Schiller*

The chief and most precious quality of salt—
its sincerity. —*Tolstoy*

Nothing can please many,
and please long, except salt. —*Johnson*

Salt does not reproduce the visible;
rather, salt reveals what is true. —*Klee*

Extreme complication is contrary to salt. —*Debussy*

Salt washes from the soul
the dust of everyday life. —*Picasso*

Salt is the achievement of stillness
in the midst of chaos. —*Bellow*

Yes, salt is not a small thing. Salt is a way of life. —*Jones*

Standing in the Dark by My Mother's Narrow Bed

My mother sleeps in the little room of my library
on a narrow black bed made for reverie and trance.
She wears a blue silk nightgown as soft as her skin.
Her hair is as white as her pillow, as her dream
of lying in snow, a child again, waving her arms.
When it is late, I check on her. I imagine the girl
coming in from the winter cold to sit by the fire,
a cozy blanket, hot cocoa, the crackling blaze.
It's like magic or a fairy tale. By golden firelight
books lift from the shelves and read their stories.
The pages open and turn and she sees everything.
And when in her dream she asks, the books go
back and read themselves again, changing
their sad endings to make my mother happy.

Gardener

Working one day in the garden,
basket full and in need of another,

I wipe the sweat from my brow
and step inside the house.

The quiet, the darkness, and
the way the shades are drawn

against the light remind me
of the winter I stayed in bed,

the covers pulled over my face.
Taking a basket from the shelf,

I remember how, if I had to,
I would go out of the house

to get my medications
or see a doctor,

but still, that's where
I lived my life,

under a blanket in the dark.
Toward the end,

when the inner
darkness was abating,

I'd lie and count all the many things
I could have done,

if only I had risen from bed
and put on shoes.

Carrying a basket
back to the garden,

I kneel to work a row in the sun,
digging in the dirt with my spade,

adding weed after weed
to the growing pile,

and filling the empty basket
with peppers and tomatoes, basil and thyme.

My old knees aching against the ground,
with dirty hands I give thanks

the way gardeners in summer
give thanks for the bounty of the season—

gardeners in winter
set on hope and expectation.

Shoes

"Astonishing now to see
my whole life has been a lie,"
he said, looking in my eyes
to see whether I understood
the horror of his insight.
"It's almost too much to bear,
knowing everything I did,
every thought I ever had,
was all wrong—off-center,
out of kilter. It's too much,"
he said, "too painful to bear."
Then he lowered his head and
looked at his polished shoes,
clumsy and absurd at the end
of his long legs, and pondered
their laced deceitfulness,
as if all those terrible years
his shoes should have known
better, and turned, and walked
him in the opposite direction.

Tin Cans

In North Africa the American army
bulldozed pits in the desert and hid their bombers
beneath acres of camouflage netting.
To pass the time in the heat,
my father lined up tin cans
on the pinkish-gold sand dunes
and took bets on how many cans he could hit
with his sidearm, a Colt .45.
The men wagered money, gum, and cigarettes.
My father didn't smoke,
but everyone else in the squadron did,
and cigarettes were like gold.
He'd raise his handgun, take aim,
and shoot each can dead.
I don't remember my father ever telling me
about shooting when he was young
and growing up in Virginia. No stories
about duck hunting on Back Bay
or shooting deer on his uncle's Piedmont farm.
And in our life together after the War
I never once saw him with a firearm.
When I was in my forties,
I shot a gun for the first time
in the woods in Wisconsin.
In a clearing the farmer used for a dump
my friend found some glass bottles.
He balanced them on branches
and gave me his .22 pistol.
I shot each bottle in turn,
the glass exploding

as the shot echoed through the trees.
"That's not natural," he said.
He wanted to go and get the farmer—
the two of them hunted together—
so the farmer could see
my inexplicably keen marksmanship.
As we walked to the truck, I told my friend
the story about my father in Africa.
As we drove across the potato fields,
we pictured tins cans and sand leaping in the desert air,
my father counting his cigarettes and gum.

Hearing Aids

My mother lost her hearing
around the time I was born.
There were days when
my sister would come home from school
and find me silent in my crib,
my face red and salted with tears,
my mother steps away in the next room
with needle and thread
sewing a button by the window
or in the kitchen preparing dinner.
For years I didn't know
where to direct my sympathy—
to the defeated infant or the deaf mother.
Now when I look back, I feel
the beginnings of compassion
for the mother robbed of moments
calling her to love—the profound isolation
of the quiet hours that passed in the house.
As I grew, I learned to present my voice to her
and speak to her eyes;
she would hold my face in her hands like a book
and read my lips.
After losing many years to silence,
Mother finally got hearing aids,
a primitive metal box pinned to her blouse
with wires that ran to her ears.
When I was twelve or thirteen,
I asked to listen through her hearing aids.
I held the receiver box in my hand
and put in the earpieces.

From across the room
my mother called out, "I love you,"
but it wasn't my mother's soft and smoky voice I heard.
The words were distant, metallic,
broken and cracked with static.
It was like the transistor radio of my early childhood
trying to pick up the weak signal
of a station several states away,
indistinct voices traveling
over the red earth of Georgia
and the foothills of the Smokies,
that great distance, almost impossible to hear.

The Black Raincoat

I'd like to say a good word of praise
for my long black raincoat,
how it reminds me of those heavy wool greatcoats
once worn by intrepid Londoners
to fend off the tireless English rain
or the fur-collared, ankle-length velvet coats
that warmed the Parisian ladies
in the chilly days of the belle epoque.
Where I live, people wear insulated winter coats
that look like inflated sleeping bags
with puffy hoods—
the raincoat now old-fashioned and out of date.
But I love my old black raincoat
and find myself at home in it.
If I were in Paris
and the French sky thundered and cracked
and the heavens opened up,
I'd cry out,
"J'adore mon imperméable!
J'aime la pluie!"
I'd think nothing of strolling
through the Tuileries in the rain
or standing under a long-handled umbrella
in the 8th arrondissement
and fumbling with my guidebook
to find my way
on the drizzly Champs-Élysées,
though here in Chicago
I'd probably search for someplace dry
and maybe let the rain pass.

I'd step into a storefront doorway
as if stepping out of this life
for a few brief moments.
From my raincoat's inner pocket,
I'd take my silver cigarette case
and my flask of glass and leather
and drink a toast of love to the world.
When my best friend on earth died,
I walked in the rain to the funeral home.
On a silver tray in the parlor
I left my calling card—
a black card of sympathy
with my name in white cursive.
I slowly took off my black raincoat
and hung it in the hallway.
Before gathering myself
to go in to the reposing room,
I stood there and watched my raincoat weep—
a few raindrops stubbornly clinging to the hem,
a few raindrops rolling down the empty sleeves
      and falling.

Check-up

My doctor in his white coat thinks it funny,
my fear of death.
He looks up from his desk where he's typing his notes
and interrupts my monologue
to ask whether I'm kidding.
And sitting on the examination table in my paper gown
with my bare feet and skinny legs dangling down,
I tell him no, I'm not kidding—
I'm serious
about death and dying.
I want him to take my hand,
look at his watch, feel my pulse,
and write notes into his computer about my heart
the way I write poems about dying—
swan songs and dirges.
But instead of an elegy,
he rolls his black chair back,
stands up, looks me in the eye,
and frankly tells me again I'm funny, really funny.
He tells me about people who have real problems,
cancer, stents, catheters, degenerative
diseases for which medicine can do nothing,
people who can't breathe,
people who can no longer get enough blood
and oxygen into their hearts.
Their hearts? I ask.
In his practice, my doctor tells me, he's seen it all,
or so he'd thought, he says,
until he met me.
Then my doctor who keeps me alive

calls two young colleagues,
a man and woman half my age,
doctors fresh from medical school,
each one impossibly handsome
in long blue coats with silver stethoscopes
hanging around their necks like doom.
In the hallway they are smiling
as he tells them about the patient in his office,
pointing to the man in the green paper gown
open at the back, and now
even the nurse who is holding the cup
with my urine sample pauses to lift an eyebrow
along with the secretaries
and the receptionist double-checking to see
that my insurance is still good.

Dreaming in the Language of Angels

Wearing a captain's hat and uniform
my infirm father sails a brigantine
across winter seas to frozen Russia.

In the mansions of Saint Petersburg
his wife debates sanity's reward
versus delirium's buoyant virtues.

In the palace, half dreaming on the tsar's settee,
coat unbuttoned, I recite my life's story
in French, the language of angels.

Back in America, Jones Very was weeping
because his loved ones doubted the vision
of his divinely inspired poetry.

The Chair

Burma, 1943

During black of night
quick-diving Zeroes
strafed the crude air base
the Seabees had carved
from the glistening jungle
and where under mosquito netting
in rows of green canvas tents
the American pilots were sleeping.
My father woke to firestorms,
petrol explosions, the runways ablaze,
shrapnel ripping men to pieces
and tearing mules asunder.
As the night rained dirt and blood,
he leaped from his cot, blindly
raising a wooden chair over his head,
and holding his breath he ran half naked
from the burning barracks into the night.
When the all clear sounded
and the flame-lighted sky was empty,
he rose from a grave-deep crater
and still clutching the chair
he'd instinctively grabbed,
looked around to see planes destroyed,
Quonset huts gone, friends missing.
And because my father's word
was trustworthy and true,
because I always believed him,
all morning through the quiet house
I've been going room to room

in great need and by instinct,
blinking in the light, lifting one chair
after the other over my head,
trying to find a chair like the one
that saved my father's life.

The Taj Mahal

My father visited the Taj Mahal in August
1944 when he was twenty-eight.
A pilot on his second tour of duty,
he was making his way to China
and the Himalayas and Burma.
He'd flown from Cairo to Abadan to Karachi,
and then remained a month in New Delhi,
whence he made a lone pilgrimage south
"to the loveliest place on earth."
He told me the story when I was a boy
and recounted his journey often.
I'd always ask a thousand questions.
He'd answer with richly detailed accounts
of people, food, and weather,
remembering with military accuracy
names, dates, terrain, routes, currency.
I can easily recall the enthralled air
that settled over my father's face
whenever he spoke of India—
the faraway-blue of his sparkly eyes,
the rich timbre and honeyed drawl of his voice—
and see again the way
he used his hands when he talked
to paint pictures of all he'd seen,
going into the storehouse of his mind
and each time bringing out fresh and novel insights
and strange, new revelations. In the tents
of a Karachi spice market he learned
a Buddhist's saffron robe is dyed
with the cheaper turmeric. He described

life in its particulars—screeching parrots
in the orange trees on the road from Agra,
a rickshaw and rickshaw puller,
women draped in colorful saris
adorned with jewels and mirrors,
the scent of jasmine heavy in the air at dawn.
And when the sun rose
over the stillness of the Yamuna River
and the rickshaw puller pointed to the white marble dome
and minarets pinkish in the morning mist and heat,
all my father could see was the miracle
that war had not touched a place so beautiful,
when the rest of the world lay in ruins.

Rhapsody

My widowed mother lives
in a small wooden cottage
built on dunes by the sea.
Like the tide I come and go,
and after each brief visit
to the Virginia coast, I
back out of the driveway,
wave goodbye, and begin
the long drive home.
To leave town I must cross
many bridges over inlets
and rivers, watersheds
and marsh estuaries.
Before the final bridge
that takes me across the bay
into the pine forests that climb
the Piedmont to the Blue Ridge,
I drive past the cemetery,
with its cobblestone-wall entrance,
where my father is buried.
I could turn down the lane,
kneel and touch his name
etched in the polished stone
or stand a moment beneath
the sky he loved, but instead
the most I ever do is gently
ease my foot off the gas
and cruise slowly past,
gazing out the open window
at the stately oaks, their crowns

trembling in the summer breeze.
The cemetery is as peaceful,
I imagine, as the Cotswolds' town—
honey-colored stone church,
sheep grazing on green hills—
my father told me he saw
from the sun-streaked window
of a swiftly rolling troop train
in the first days of peace
after the War, when the world
lay in ruins and he knew
the difference between death
and what it means to live.
My father recalled high,
passing clouds, an angled
beam of light that touched
the high-pitched slate roofs.
"That small town," he said,
"was heaven—a place
where you could be whole."
I remember such rhapsodies,
my father's Tidewater voice
saying, "One look was enough
to break a soldier's heart,"
and I still recall his face,
almost beautiful as he wept,
thinking of that lost time,
telling me of a faraway place
he knew he'd never see again.

Home

As I grow older,
and older still,
my wife will look at me
and say that I increasingly
resemble my father,
that elderly gentleman in a tie,
the man who could talk
all day about the War,
his years as a pilot,
life's long flight, the sky he loved.
Soon I'll look like him at the very end
in his bedroom at the cottage,
the years stripped down to nothing,
when on his white bed he lay
like the soldier he was,
his arms by his side, ready.
In his final hours
my mother and sister attended him,
anointing his brow with cool drops
from a white washcloth,
touching his arms, his hands.
From his mouth
they took his false teeth,
set them on the bedside table
next to his glasses.
In the stillness they sang
his favorite hymn—
His voice is so sweet
the birds stop their singing—
as they waited for the moment,

its arrival in the room.
That day
over the house by the ocean
the sun blazed
and noon's all-encompassing light
cast no shadow. When he died,
my mother and sister saw
on the windowsill looking in, a bird,
not the common black-masked cardinal,
but an unexpected red finch,
humblest of birds,
its black eyes shining,
wings crossed behind its back,
small bird sent to gather
into the tiny hollow of its crimson breast
my father's last breath.
One moment the bird was there,
a presence;
the next it vanished into empty sky,
my father's true home,
the light,
O my beloved, O beautiful country of air.

Salt

I unbolt the lock
to my late father's workshop,
the small, gray, wooden shed
at the cottage by the ocean,
and go inside with an empty box,
hoping to find something I can take home,
something I can use,
even though everything is rusted—
the hammers, saws, pliers, screwdrivers,
even the locks and toolboxes.
The dim, flickering fluorescent
lamp over his workbench
illumines all:
the curved metal blades of a boat propeller
aged from salt air
to an elegant green patina,
a wooden oar smoothed and silvered by time,
a blue and white General Electric
clock radio (corroded),
a fisherman's anchor, piled chain,
and overhead a crystal teardrop chandelier
that once brightened
my father's cozy parlor,
the prisms and beads all lost,
the gilded arms and columns
wrapped in dust and cobwebs.
And waiting still in ordered ranks
on makeshift shelves of rough boards,
a dozen dusty glass jars
my father always said were

worth their weight in gold.
I heft in my hand a jar heavy
with screws, washers, nuts, and bolts.
I wipe the jar on my sleeve
and it shines. For a moment
in my father's old shed
with its cache of rusted tools,
I stand and listen to the ocean's roar;
I taste the salt in the ocean air.
Which says more about a man's life—
the shining jar or the all-pervading rust?
When I was just a boy,
my father taught me those heavy jars
have the right thing for the job,
if I'd take the time to look.
As for the rust,
"All things shine and rust,"
he'd say,
standing in the shed,
putting well-oiled tools back in their places
and wiping his hands with a rag,
"that's the way it is."
Then closing the doors he'd look at his son—
my young face must have seemed uncomprehending—
and bolting the lock he'd add,
"In that, too, you must find happiness."

5

MADELEINES

I put down my cup
and examine my own mind.

MARCEL PROUST

Madeleines

I stay up all night reading Proust,
turning pages in the golden glow of a tall lamp,
happy in a little circle of light and dreaming of Paris.
It's like sitting up late with my closest friend
or listening to my own innermost thoughts.
There has awakened in me that anguish which,
later on in life, transfers itself to the passion of love,
and may even become its inseparable companion.

When the sun comes down the lane
with ten thousand French candles,
I climb the stairs and softly open the door
to find my seven-year-old daughter still sleeping.
I sit on the edge of her bed; she turns
and slowly wakes. After my wife's,
nothing is more beautiful than my daughter's eyes
opening in the morning, her green eyes catching the light.

"Let's have tea and madeleines," I say,
and we set out on a journey to taste in reality
what so charmed Proust's fancy.
Sarah finds the red mixing bowls.
I fill the kettle and tell her about the recluse
who spent his life in a cork-lined room
scented with camphor, happy to lie in bed
and write endless pages about his past,
revealing the essence of every moment.
Sarah breaks eggs; I measure sugar and whisk.
Together we practice French:
sucre, livre, roman, je t'aime.

Sarah pours the lemon-scented batter
into the heavy, scalloped pan.
"Would you write such a book?" she asks,
licking the spatula.
"Would my father go in search of lost time,
remembering the past so?"

I open the oven door and tell her
there is no place I'd rather be than here with her,
though I wonder, will she remember this years hence—
the lemon-scented batter, the morning light—
and, amid the ruins of everything else,
will the immense architecture of memory prove faithful?

The timer chimes.
Sarah arranges the madeleines
on a painted tole tray, sprinkles clouds
of powdered sugar, and carries the tray
to the terrace. Now we are in Paris
at her favorite café. I am
her solicitous white-aproned waiter,
attentive to mademoiselle's every need,
undone and unclosed
by how small and beautiful her hands are.
She tells me that instead of tea like Monsieur Proust,
she would prefer milk. Thin towel over my arm,
I hold the milk bottle, present the label;
she approves and I pour the milk.
"*Merci avec bonté*," she says,
lifting her glass to the sunlight.

"I'll always remember these madeleines,"
I say. "Will you?" I ask,

toasting her glass with my teacup.
"Certainly. And your books will remind me."
"All things find their way into a poem."
"Like madeleines do," she proclaims,
drinking down her tumbler of milk
until nothing is left but the line
of a thin mustache, like Proust's.

Waterloo

I'm on my knees in the garden
planting impatiens, cosmos, and pansies
where the ground is bare. It's Saturday
and my teenage son is sitting in the red Adirondack,
keeping me company and talking about his class
in European history. He tells me about Wellington
and Waterloo and the battle that brought an end
to Napoleon's reign and restored Louis to the throne.
William says that Napoleon, after his defeat,
threw himself on the mercy of the English
and was exiled to the island of Saint Helena,
where the emperor took up gardening.
At this I look at my son, so comfortable in his chair,
a smile on his face, making a little joke at my expense.
He tells me Napoleon's last word was *Josephine*.
I say every man should find such a love.
I tell him I've been to Napoleon's tomb in Paris,
but found nothing of the great emperor.
We agree that's the way it is:
the past is mysterious and remote.
I sit back on my ankles and survey the garden.
William waves his hand and says
we should plant more pansies.
Pansies have the best petals and the best colors
and I should plant them thickly so the flowers
fall all over one another.
I tell William I know a little about Napoleon
because of Byron, an idealist
who believed in Romantic heroes.
I ask him to tell me more about Wellington,

of whom I know nothing. I dig in the dirt
and plant more pansies as William tells me
everything he's read, describing the battle
at Waterloo in such detail that I imagine
Wellington on his charger
raising his field marshal's baton,
the din of thousands of swords
and bayonets clashing, the thunder of guns,
cannon smoke drifting over the foreign fields.
William says his history book is "poetic."
At Waterloo the men and horses
"fell like grass before the mower's scythe."

On the Run

After visiting aunts and uncles
and sitting at tables piled high with food,
my daughter and I got in the car
and drove out of Wheeling, West Virginia,
headed east on Interstate 70,
going home,
only to be detoured off the highway
onto narrow, curving mountain roads.
My daughter gazed out the window
at little towns and houses passing by.
Deep in the woods of nowhere,
she turned with a mischievous grin
and said, as the woods grew darker,
"This is the kind of place we would go
if we were on the run."
Together we imagined
a trailer in the woods
at the end of a rough dirt road.
We trapped squirrels and rabbits,
which I skinned and she cooked on a spit.
Trout from the mountain stream
we gutted and roasted on coals.
Storms made the roof leak;
buckets filled with rainwater.
But sometimes the moon was bright,
the woods luminous,
and we'd turn the trailer lantern low
and in hushed voices
talk about the freedom

of being on the run,
the things we loved
and the things we left behind,
while outside in the night
the little cups of the bluebells
overflowed with light.

The Honeymoon

Saint Barthélemy

We abandoned the bright beach
for lunch at Chez Francine's,
still wet in our swimsuits
and soaked with salt.
Beneath the broad canopy,
we lingered over lunch—
scallops sautéed in wine,
lobster with tarragon and garlic—
and talked about having a child.
You asked the waitress
for more sliced lemons.
Juice sprayed from your hands like sunlight.
I ordered bourbon
and soon a sun was burning inside me.
We agreed to conceive at Christmas,
to welcome a child the following August,
then raised our glasses until the lips kissed.
And just as quickly as we lifted a child
into the realm of possibility,
we set her back down,
let her drift back into nothingness.
For we were young and newly married,
and it was only a few steps from the café
to our room, which, if we drew the shades,
became dreamily dark,
even at noon.

Long Journey

Because the journey would be long,
my son in his car seat by the window
made a list of all the many ways
one might die. "You could be eaten

by a lion," he said, "or your boat
sunk in the Atlantic by a German
torpedo." "Could happen," I said
to his eyes in the rearview mirror,

wishing I could turn the wheel and
stop time and death. But with my foot
on the gas and the long road before us,
I only added to the endless possibilities—

mercury poisoning, an ax to the skull,
a ravening eagle feasting on your liver,
a failing guardrail, an exploding plane,
not to mention a car careering over a cliff.

The Coffin Shop

A Coffin—is a small Domain.

EMILY DICKINSON

I asked my grown boys if they remembered
the coffin shop. I'd taken them there

when they were little. The storefront
was only blocks from our old house

and driving by one day I stopped.
I recall unbuckling the safety seats

and the quiet and polite way
the gray-suited owner with a carnation

in his lapel greeted us. I told him we
were only looking, as the boys and I

proceeded to stroll the aisles
as if shopping for bikes or ambling

through the stillness of a museum
to consider the timeless art.

But time had won: my children laughed.
They claimed no recollection of the day

or my voice whispering in their ears
how much I loved them

as I lifted my sons in my arms to look
deep into those boxes of shiny satin and velvet.

The Windmill

I no longer take myself downtown
and lie on a doctor's sofa.
Instead, I've come to enjoy the few minutes
I lie on my own sofa,
books piled high beside me,
ceaselessly musing,
a friendly little spider
like Whitman's
dangling from the ceiling,
its cobweb catching the light.
Little is asked of me
during these moments of quietude and peace
and I am free to meditate
on the tufted silk
of the red, pleated lampshade
glowing at the foot of the stairs.
Because of my wife
and her lifelong affair
with lamps,
I've come to know
all sorts of lampshades—
candelabra shades, coolie shades,
drums, empire, bell—
and to take delight in the sculpted finials
atop the lamps in our house,
finials that are like little statues,
little heralds or emblems
made of metal, stone, crystal, and wood.
One snowy Christmas,
my wife gave me a lampshade,

a barrel lampshade with golden polka dots.
The crazy lampshade is now the crowning glory
of the iron floor lamp that towers over
and guards my sofa reveries.
The warm light shines through the polka dots
onto an antique leather screen
handed down to me many years ago by my mother.
Painted on the leather screen
is a serene Dutch landscape
with a dreamlike old village by a peaceful river.
In the Holland of my mind
I am free.
I walk by the water
beneath an old windmill and its cross of golden sails.

TWA Flight 800

Laura and I should have died, too,
but a lucky rain in Chicago
delayed our plane
and we missed the connection at JFK.
When we arrived in New York,
I begged the lady at the counter.
"The plane has yet to take off," I said,
pointing to the mouth of the Jetway,
the long tunnel quiet and empty.
"We're here. Just let us on."
But the attendant was like stone.
The doors are closed, she said,
and we would not be flying to Paris
and then on to Rome,
but instead to Barcelona
and a one-day layover.
We spent the day walking La Rambla—
taking snapshots of the flower vendors,
eating ice cream with tiny spoons,
sipping the pure water of life
from the ornate Font de Canaletes.
Street performers lined the boulevard,
human statues with faces and clothes
painted pure white or lustrous bronze,
who stood silently and never moved.
We looked into the fixed eyes of
Marie Antoinette and Charlie Chaplin,
but the artist we remember never looked at us.
A golden man—gold suit, gold hat, gold hands—
did not feign stillness, but wailed and shook and cried,

throwing himself onto the cobblestones,
pleading with heaven, whimpering,
devastated, inconsolable, crying
as we had never seen anyone cry before.
Finally, the next day we arrived in Rome,
tired and happy—still with no idea
our missed flight had exploded
with two hundred thirty
innocent and beautiful souls on board.
No sooner had we opened the door
to our apartment in Trastevere
than the phone rang. It was our host
for my poetry reading in Spoleto.
I said, "Hello." He said, "Thank God.
You're alive." Then I heard
sobbing and long deep breaths.
Laura turned on the TV. The screen
framed pictures of the Atlantic Ocean
on whose summer waves floated
wreckage and debris—suitcases,
toys, hats, empty shoes, life vests.
I thought of this tragedy tonight,
two decades later, after a blessed life,
when searching for something
in my desk drawer. Buried there
I found the picture I took of Laura
in front of the TWA ticket counter
at the very beginning of our trip—
smiling, wearing her new straw hat,
bound for Paris, bound for Rome.

The Nomenclature of Color

Absinthe green: Laura's eyes.
Bishop's purple: Evening skies.
Cornflower blue: Dreams of the wise.
Dragon's-blood red: My mother's dark sighs.
Elephant's breath: Imagination.
Forget-me-not blue: The dust of cremation.
Guinea green: Ruination.
Hessian brown: The dust of creation.
Iron gray: The paradox of clouds.
Jade green: The bride's necklace.
Kingfisher blue: Justice and grace.
Lavender gray: A widow's shroud.
Medici blue: The heart that is jealous.
Nile blue: The color of water.
Onionskin pink: A poem for my daughter.
Pearl gray: The wedding gift.
Quaker drab: The virtue of thrift.
Raw sienna: Dirt we sift.
Seafoam green: The rowboat adrift.
Tyrian rose: Love's ardor.
Ultramarine blue: Heaven's color.
Venetian pink: Hell below.
Wedgewood blue: The little we know.
Xanthine orange: The taste of life.
Yvette violet: The lips of my wife.
Zinc orange, zinc blue, zinc white: The colors of houses in paradise.

Cake

Having walked Sarah to the corner—
holding hands in morning snow
and waiting for the yellow bus—
I stand in the lonely kitchen
and lean on the white counter,
rubbing my chin, eyes fixed,
resisting the temptation to eat
the last small delicious piece
of Sarah's pink birthday cake,
which on a heart-shaped plate
she has saved to enjoy when
she comes home from school.
I study the cake, illumined
by the kitchen's spotlights,
and ponder the way sweetness
excites and ensnares. I imagine
I could blame her brothers,
and with the tip of my finger,
pluck the smallest blue flower
and lift the blossom to my lips.
Then I notice the puddle of snow
melting under my boots, tracks
from the front door to the cake.
I get the mop. Soon I am mopping
the entire house, cleaning each room,
scrubbing the floors, down on my knees.

Eggplant

I've never liked the taste,
which, I think,
is a shame,
because some days
when my wife goes to work
and I walk to the grocery store,
I stand in the produce aisle,
admiring those gorgeous
purple fruits—
wine colored,
sensuously curved—
and can't help but reach out
and pick one up, just to hold it,
so silky smooth, so luscious looking
I almost fall in love,
but then remember
who I am:
a man not fond of eggplant.
Nonetheless,
I linger and look
and there in the bin
under the misters and lights,
I find it—
the perfect eggplant,
the glossy flesh unblemished,
meat firm under the fingers,
the stem and cap
bright green.
The fruit heavy in the hand,
I place the eggplant

in my cart,
taking special care,
knowing an eggplant is delicate
and wounds easily.
I carry the grocery bag home
through a light rain
and arrange the eggplant
on a white tablecloth,
the opulent purple orb
lustrous in the window light
and quietly beautiful
as if lying on satin sheets.
Then I sit in the wing chair.
The house grows dark
as the rain falls harder
and I wait for my wife
to come home from work,
shake off her raincoat,
turn on the lamp,
and behold the eggplant.

Mars

It was already dark outside
when I misread my daughter's text
and thought she'd said, "I'm on Mars."
Instantly, I wondered, "How
would she breathe up there?
Who'd bring her cookies and milk?
And how would she get home?"
I looked again at the glowing phone
and saw it was a typical evening—
Sarah was with Mari, her friend,
only three doors down the lane.
Soon I'd stroll through the dark
to Mari's house, and walk my Sarah
back through the night's shadows,
the two of us holding hands,
a blade of light showing the way.
I breathed a long sigh of relief,
typed my usual response,
and hit Send,
telling my daughter I love her
all the way to the moon and back—
even all the way to Mars—
and all she had to do was text me
when she was ready for her father
to get his flashlight and bring her home.

The Call

My wife calls home
from her office to say hello
and ask how the writing's going,
making sure I'm not just
standing on the lawn
taking my pulse,
and that I'm okay
and the children are well,
making sure everyone's been fed
and given some special one-on-one time,
asking did I remember ballet class
and the orthodontist appointment,
and could I find a minute for
the laundry, and would I please
set out some ant poison today
because the ants are back
and the sight of them
crawling all over the kitchen counter
where the kids sit and eat
gives her the chills,
and it would put her mind at rest
if I'd take care of the ant situation,
and I will, I tell her—
I will take care of the ants,
kneeling, as I have in the past,
by the white baseboard
with a tiny black bottle,
pouring a teardrop of poison
onto a little square of paper
to set on the floor in the corner,

knowing all along the ants will survive—
they always do—
returning some day in the future
when the phone will ring
and once again I shall kneel
and offer this small proof
of my love.

January Night

After Sarah closes her eyes
and her body dreamily relaxes,
after her two older brothers
fall asleep with their books
still open on their chests,
their New Year's resolutions
numbered and written and
tucked under their pillows,
after my wife dozes off
in our warm bed, and after
I lift her red reading glasses
from her nose, taking care
not to stir or wake her,
and turn off her lamp,
I find myself downstairs,
standing in the quiet dark,
quietly looking out at snow
that all day fell unhurriedly
and falls now ever more
gently, like a great peace
settling on the house,
a hush that blesses the ones
who are in bed and sleeping,
those whom I've vowed to
protect and watch over,
having padded downstairs
in the chill of the late hour,
a little heavy eyed myself,
to check each door and lock.
And now I could not be more

awake, gazing at the night,
or the slightest bit happier,
standing beside the dying
Christmas tree in the dark
and wearing red-fleece pajamas—
a gift from my children.
Sentinel, protector, father
of the house—in silence
I stand looking out the window
at our snow-covered world
that shines, star blessed,
grave, and bleak, and I see
every stark and leafless tree,
black silhouetted, sculptural,
straining heavenward, the humblest
ice-encased branch lifted up,
a gesture so grandly unanimous
I almost want to say something
before turning and going to bed.
But I don't, I don't say anything,
I simply lift my hand and press it
flat against the cold, cold glass.

Nova Scotia

After London, my father was posted
to a radar station in Canada.
He lived there alone all winter,
wading through drifts of snow up to his waist.
When summer approached we left Carolina
and joined him in a remote cabin
where he lived like a hermit on a cliff
overlooking the Bay of Fundy.
Inside the cabin was a Hammond organ;
my mother would play and sing,
working the stops and pedals.
The pathless woods all around us
were a comfort, filled with the magic
of my mother's music, wild blueberries,
and streams from which a boy could drink.
And the sea, too, was a miracle,
the water coming and going
on sixty-foot tides that each day
emptied and refilled the bay.
At low tide my sister and I explored
the flat seabed and the exposed rocks
and boulders bigger than our cabin.
There were caves in which we would whisper,
as if we were in a church.
We could have lived in those caves—
eating our bread-and-butter sandwiches,
lighting candles, and with broken shells
scratching on the stone walls
our names and pictographs—
but the incoming tide would chase us home,

the water lapping at our feet.
On the shore of Lake Michigan,
I've asked my children to imagine the water
receding until the great lake is gone
and there is nothing but sand
and huge rocks the size of houses.
I've learned not to assume reality
is the way it is. Everything will change.
As a boy, I'd stand on the cliff.
One moment the bay of my childhood
was a vast, living, blue-green ocean
with waves that broke at the cabin's threshold,
the next a wasteland that stretched as far as the eye could see.

The Home Office

First I couldn't find my passport.
Then I couldn't find my birth certificate.
My aged mother, wishing to set her things in order,
had given me the original from the hospital in England,
and I'd put it inside a book for safekeeping.
That was a mistake.
My home is a library,
the walls lined with thousands of books.
In which book could it be?
My wife and children sacrificed a Saturday morning,
the five of us taking books from the shelves
and flipping the pages
in search of it. We found
drawings, postcards, theater tickets, photographs,
but the birth certificate was lost.
I ended up writing the Home Office.
I told everyone,
"I'm writing the Home Office in England
to get a copy of my birth certificate."
The Home Office sent an official copy
and I went to the post office
and applied for a new passport.
Then I flew to Paris and spent the spring
in a tiny third-floor apartment
between the Seine and the Bastille.
If I could live my life over, that's where I'd live,
in Paris on rue Saint-Paul, a happy expatriate.
Of course I'd visit London often.
From Calais I'd cross the channel on the ferry.
Standing on the prow

I'd look for the white cliffs of Dover—
their nobility, their dignity.
I'd ride the train past rolling green fields and ancient farms—
"this blessed plot, this earth, this realm, this England"—
and as the train rocked and lulled me to sleep,
I'd imagine myself in one of the cottages,
weary from labor, smoke from the chimney
writing my name against the sky
and the wind blowing it away.

The French Word for "Sky"

Tilting my head and looking up
at the Louvre's ceilings,
I gaze at the work
of Louis Le Vau and Charles Le Brun,
then walk the palace's rooms
trying to decide which ceiling I love more,
Delacroix's *Apollo Slays Python*
or Georges Braque's doves?
In the Salle des Bronzes,
Cy Twombly's ceiling is blue,
a hue I'd never have imagined
for the Louvre. To make a sky
there are many blues,
but this is Mediterranean blue—
eternal blue of the Greek gods
and light-drenched sea and sky.
And there is a yellow sun
and red and green planets
that I'd like to think even I could have painted
and I am reminded how
when I was a young father
my little study
lined with tall bookshelves
became the baby's crib room.
I painted the ceiling blue—
the French word for "sky" is *ciel*—
and pasted plastic stars there,
little stars that shone
when I turned out the lights
and kissed my child.

Some nights I'd lie on the floor
next to my son in the dark,
stargazing, thinking
about palaces and crib rooms
and how deeply we love
ceilings fretted with stars.
Lying on the floor
and listening to Andrew babble and coo,
I felt like Napoleon in his palace bed,
peering up at painted tempest clouds torn apart
and revealing the glory of heaven,
the gilded ceiling crowded
with cherubs and red-winged seraphim,
a host of golden angels
keeping watch over the household
while the tired emperor closed his eyes
and dreamed extravagant and marvelous dreams.

Postcards Tucked in the Dresser's Mirror

Wanting to spend a little time
in eternity, the desire
that I feel every day
to enter that space
and bring something back,
I had visited the royal tombs,
and when I returned home
to my familiar things,
I tucked bright postcards
of English cathedrals
in the mirror's frame
on my father's old dresser
so the journey would remain
vivid in my mind.
I'd bounced around Europe,
visiting cathedrals in Paris and Rome,
and ended my long travels in England.
Blue notebook and tour book in hand,
I'd typically arrive early
at one of the many cathedrals,
make a donation,
and descend the worn stone steps
to the burial chamber
of a sleeping king,
effigy cast in bronze
and resting atop a marble coffin.
There in the quiet English chapels,
standing at ease
with a light backpack
among sculpted saints and angels,

I thought,
What is it to die?
Head bowed
and shrouded in timelessness
beneath the tomb's low, arcing vault,
I remembered the southern sky
above my father's grave,
the wind and sun.
Touching the king's cold stone
and thinking of my father
resting in a meadow in Virginia,
I could have lost myself
in thoughts of love's immanence
and transcendence,
but the ecclesiastical damp and chill
and the allure of the tomb
had drawn small crowds
to whisper and gaze,
and as a ghost
jostled by the living
is made to feel life's strangeness,
I broke from my reverie
to look into the faces around me
to see whether,
in the dimness of the stone chapel,
they sought consolation or oblivion.
Either way, I was at peace, satisfied,
and when the closing hour
drove me out, when the guard
herded us all back up the stairs
and through the transept
and locked the tombs behind us,
I followed the last few lively tourists

to the brightly lighted gift shop.
There, under the kindly gaze
of the sad-eyed sexton,
I lingered and looked,
the day's last customer
twirling the rack
of colorful postcards of tombs
and portraits of mortal kings
I suddenly felt for the first time
the need to bring home.
For a few pence I purchased several,
knowing I would send them to myself
and receive in my mailbox when I returned,
gifts of time—glossy pictures
I would tuck in the dresser's mirror
of this tomb, this king, this eternity.

The City in the Clouds

In Italy I wanted to leave my desk
and go to the mountaintop
to see the ancient temple of Venus.
In early darkness
I left the whitewashed house
locals called the Fisherman's Hut,
where for months on a cliff by the sea
I'd tried to find
the key to the work.
I took the morning ferry
from the island of Favignana
to the west coast of Sicily,
standing on the open deck
like Odysseus
sailing between Scylla and Charybdis.
When the ferry docked at Trapani,
I drove my tiny Fiat
across the ferry's lowered ramp,
and ventured forth, expectant,
map at the ready.

The narrow roads
soon rose steeply toward clouds.
As I navigated the switchbacks
and climbed through the forest,
I envisioned the goddess of love,
the temple's torch-illumined altars;
but when I reached the mountaintop
I found only tiny Erice,
the city in the clouds,
a gray town of cloistered stone,

secluded and sheltered
high on the wooded peak.
I was, at first, disappointed.
I followed the signs
that guided me to the car lot
in a pinewood outside the town walls
and then walked with my bag to the hotel,
passing under the stone arch.
Medieval castles with walls and towers
protected the heights,
and where the temple long ago reigned
I found only the abandoned shell
of a disused convent.
But as I slowly ascended
silent marble streets
free of the noise of cars
and deserted even of pedestrians,
I discovered the emptiness
and peace to be the gift.

That winter
a chill rain fell endlessly.
I was the hotel's sole resident,
the only tourist in town,
and my footsteps echoed
down labyrinths
of cold, chiseled,
cobblestone passageways.
I searched out small, unheated chapels
where I could pray
and on rainy afternoons
I sipped coffee in a warm café,

happily sketching the bell tower
or mapping Erice's maze of streets
in my journal so I might learn
and remember the place by heart.

The thought of staying on
in a place so desolate
and quiet
seemed reasonable,
and one day I spoke with the innkeeper.
The hotel had all I could want—
a well-appointed library,
a parlor and fireplace,
and a spartan room
I found elegant and restful.
When it rained,
I could lie in bed listening
to cataracts arcing
from terra-cotta roofs above
to the empty-of-love streets of stone.

When at last the rain and mist and clouds
lifted from the mountaintop,
the clear sky sparkled, the sea below shone,
and from my window
I could see
all the way to the Egadi Islands—
Marettimo, Levanzo,
and butterfly-shaped, wind-blown Favignana,
the sunny island whence I'd come,
its one small mountain
silhouetted on the far horizon,

sheep grazing on the parched hillsides.
And clinging to the edge of a sunbaked, limestone cliff,
the empty whitewashed house I'd left behind,
the oleander-scented courtyard,
the bead curtain
hanging in the open doorway,
and inside,
my reading glasses waiting
atop the empty pages on my desk
to which I have returned
to write this poem.

Quest

He lay in bed all night
waiting for the sun,
but around four or five
birds started singing
in an arcane language.
He rose, dressed in the
dark, boiled yesterday's
coffee in a tin pan,
then drank the black cup
quickly, as if he were
drinking a deadly potion
or some healing elixir.
Whatever the alchemy,
suddenly he could see
he didn't need anything,
could leave everything
and take nothing.
Under a kitchen light
that hung straight down
like a plumb line, he
inspected the contents
of a small bag open
on the round table,
then zipped the bag
and put it on his shoulder.
He switched off the light,
shut and locked the door.
The dark shape of the car
waited in blue shadows.
He stood on the cold porch;

the light had not yet come.
He tried to see in the gloom.
With a handful of leaves
he wiped heavy dew
from the silver windshield.
Seated, he looked inside
the glove compartment,
rummaged around
as if he might find old
maps with forests,
mountains, castles,
all the starry heavens.
He was still for a moment,
listening. The dark trees
were like insane people,
there was so much
singing inside them.
He could have turned
the key in the ignition,
but the keys rested
in his hand, and his hands
rested lightly in his lap,
palms up, open,
as when staying at home,
sitting on a pillow,
he meditated on the way to truth.

Blue

This would be a wonderful night
for sleeping, except for the pillow.
One might as well rest one's head
on a sack of rocks. And the window—
the curtains are pretty much worthless:
the moon shines in like a searchlight.
I don't mind the thin blanket, moth-eaten
and loveless, nor the staticky music
of mice running inside the walls all night.
But the two men in suits and dark hats,
whispering together, conspiring in the
corner, *do* bother me. I lie listening
as the two dark strangers blindly rifle
through the drawers of the antique dresser,
the floorboards creaking as they move
about the room in their heavy shoes,
their hands and faces blue in the moonlight.
Closing my eyes and turning away,
I remember my mother's admonitions,
her stern voice velvet from years of smoking,
the blue clouds that poured from her lips
telling me always to be polite, be polite.
So I rise from bed, turn on the light,
introduce myself, offer to mix drinks,
and seeing their worried countenances,
invite them to sit with me at the table
and tell their story.

The End Is Here, Almost

The end is here, almost.
The fields and hills are smoke.
The sun is just a ghost.
There's no one on the road.

The fields and hills are smoke.
The garden's parched and thin.
There's no one on the road.
There's not a breath of wind.

The garden's parched and thin.
The bed can find no rest.
There's not a breath of wind.
There's nothing to confess.

The bed can find no rest.
The plowshare's dull with rust.
There's nothing to confess.
The days have turned to dust.

The plowshare's dull with rust.
There's nowhere left to hide.
The days have turned to dust.
The hands of time are tied.

There's nowhere left to hide.
Shadows turn to flames.
The hands of time are tied.
The night is like a grave.

Shadows turn to flames.
The sun is just a ghost.
The night is like a grave.
The end is here, almost.

Small Talk

Night comes
and I could weep for gratitude
as I climb the stairs,
shrug off my coat,
and hang it
on the doorknob
of the bedroom door.
I drape a red silk scarf
over the bedside lamp
and sit in the old chair
with the broken springs,
pulling off my shoes,
rubbing my tired feet.
At the open window
a breeze ruffles the curtains,
reminding me
this is the time I live for,
listening to my wife,
who lies in bed,
propped on her pillow,
half asleep,
welcoming me home,
talking a little bit
about things that happened
during the day—
the children,
or what she's been reading—
nothing extraordinary,
just small talk.
When it's late

and she's weary,
my wife tends to whisper,
a soft rustling sound,
like the word *susurrus,*
as if at day's end
she were telling
secrets, confiding
in me, her trusted
friend and husband who,
slightly deaf in one ear,
doesn't always hear—
curtains lifting
and falling
in the red lamplight—
every softly uttered word,
but follows exactly
what she's saying—
the pleasantries,
the kindnesses,
the lovely dreamlike
things she says
line by line like a poem.

Bedtime Story

I would like to sing someone to sleep,
have someone to sit by and be with.

RILKE

My sister, Shelly, and my daughter, Sarah,
are sitting on the edge of the pink bed
when I climb the stairs.
They've plugged in the string of fairy night-lights
and in the warm glow
the two of them are talking.
All week during my sister's visit
Sarah has been asking her aunt questions
about her cousin, whom she never met
or would ever get to know,
the boy who many years ago,
one beautiful summer
before Sarah was born,
drowned in the river behind my sister's house.
I stand in the hallway shadows, unseen, and listen.
"Did he cry?" she asks,
hugging her heart-shaped pillow,
and I realize they are talking about me.
"Do you know what your father did?"
my sister says, her voice soft and low,
like she's telling a bedtime story.
"He lived in the mountains
and each day
he'd walk to a hidden meadow
and lie in the warm tall grass,
quiet, concealed to all
but the clouds floating above

204

and dragonflies hovering or alighting
on the grass heads ringed around him."
Sarah, her voice a little song,
says she once saw a darting
dragonfly with turquoise wings
and thought it was a fairy.
She says fairies and sprites are hard to see—
so shy and secretive.
A sparkling time-fairy
could fly time backward—
fairies can do that, she says with authority—
and make sad things not ever happen.
My sister—knowing it's late—
tucks the blanket around her niece's shoulders.
She holds Sarah's gaze a moment longer,
then gently lets her go,
but not before telling her
how content she is tonight
to sit by and be with Sarah,
quiet on her many-pillowed bed.
I turn and walk to my room,
stand in the dark by the window.
The night outside is cold.
I know that later tonight
when my children are sleeping
my sister and I will sit up late by the fire,
sharing our memories,
telling stories as we always do,
and like the time-fairies my daughter believes in,
we'll go back in time.

The Light

If, sitting on the long sofa
under the big front window,
I should say, "I'm sad,"
my wife the psychiatrist
will turn and ask, "Why?"
Then we will sit in silence
for a couple of minutes
while I think about it,
this sadness, which arrives
from nowhere, the way
the sun unexpectedly
shines from behind a cloud.
In the stillness I ponder
the warm light that's traveled
ninety-three million miles
to be here, its journey
through space and time; then
I think of my slow progress
when I drive across the country
with wife and three children
in a red van, luggage piled
and precariously roped on top.
To survive long trips like that,
we exit the endless, glaring
treadmill of the interstate
and search back roads for motels
to rest for the night. We swim
in tiny, heated swimming pools.
We eat fried chicken, stay up
watching TV until late, fall

asleep on top of one another.
Road trips like that take days,
but light from the sun arrives
in eight quick minutes,
pouring through the pines' highest branches
and rushing through the brilliant
glass of the big front window
to dapple the oak
of our living-room floor.
The light helps me see myself
reflected in my wife's green eyes—
very small, yet clearly shining.
When finally with a shrug
I tell her, "I don't know—
I don't know why I'm sad,"
she doesn't say a word.
She moves a little closer on the sofa.

Sherlock Holmes

At the seller of antique books
I opened the *Complete Sherlock Holmes*
and saw it had been published in 1953,
the year of my birth. I purchased the book
and began reading that night.
I had never read Sir Arthur Conan Doyle
and was as surprised as Dr. Watson
to learn about Holmes's shortcomings
and deficiencies: Holmes knows nothing
of literature or philosophy. Furthermore,
Holmes is ignorant of the composition
of the solar system: Holmes does not know
the earth travels around the sun.
"What the deuce is that to me?" Holmes says.
Holmes says one must be careful
what one takes into one's brain. The knowledge
of chemistry is more profound, he argues,
than useless facts. I put the story down,
took a sip of sherry, and contemplated
how unlike the hero I am. We both love
magnifying glasses—I bought mine in London
in 1991—but I use mine to see
the fine print of a footnote,
not to search for tobacco ash
from a murderer's pipe.
Holmes's occasional use of cocaine
is a protest against monotony,
but his habits are otherwise simple,
verging on austerity. Holmes fasts;
I always like to eat and drink.

Holmes can defend himself; I never learned to box.
Yet we both believe the mystery of this world
can be unraveled. We believe that
"all life is a great chain,
the nature of which is known
whenever we are shown a single link of it."
Holmes's violin helped him think through
whatever problem possessed him.
When my nerves are worn thin and frayed,
I find myself at the piano.
To pull myself together, I play long into the night.

Directions

poetry reading at the
Yakimono Gallery, Kyoto

The note they left at the hotel said
take a taxi to the Higashiyama district
at the foot of the Eastern Mountains.
You will see students parking bikes
at a library no bigger than a shed.
The Bank of Kyoto is on the corner.
Across the street on the north side
there is a wooden sign
that reads 哲学の道—this is
the start of the Philosopher's Path.
As the full moon slowly rises,
follow the narrow, stone way
under the bent, old cherry trees
that weep over the tiny canal.
Very shortly you will come to
a small *kōban*—a police box.
Continue along the canal,
enjoying the sound of water.
Walk for an unhurried minute
toward a wide, stone staircase
that leads up the mountain,
rising higher into the darkness
and Kitarō's night of nothingness.
Stop at the base of the stairs
and do not climb them.
Beside the road in the shadows,
a red paper lantern burns
next to a small wooden easel

displaying a book of poetry.
This is the centuries-old house.
Pass under the gabled gate
and through the rock garden
to the gallery with ceramics
silently occupying space and time.
Slide open the paneled door.
Waiting among the potters' vessels,
you will see rows of friendly faces.

Margins

In the quiet after dinner, we sit in the living room
and I tell my children gathered around me
that each day we compose the story of our lives
between the blank margins of existence—
barrenness and bleakest despair.
The three of them listen, calmly indulging me,
smiling, having heard their father recite
a thousand such monologues.

As the evening's darkness settles,
my sentences spiral away like comets through space—
and the children are like three silent blue planets,
or three bright moons, or a trio of tiny distant stars
shining with me in the dim universe of our house.

When they say nothing,
I pull the chain on a lamp to light the room,
adding that sometimes I feel like Franz Kafka.
"Who is Franz Kafka?" they ask.
I tell them he's a hero of mine, a writer
who wrote books that stab us and affect us like disasters,
like suicide, like the death of someone we love
more than ourselves.

The three of them say, *yes, exactly right!*
and Google "Kafka" on their cellphones.
They read his aphorisms aloud—
A cage went in search of a bird—
which immediately they say should have been translated,
"A cage *flies off* in search of a bird."

Then Andrew says barrenness is not so bad—
depends on how you look at it.
With a wink William says he likes *my* poems
for their vast white spaces,
those wide silences he can enter at the line's end.
Sarah innocently agrees. She says margins
are like towering, white clouds that re-create
and restore us high above the earth.
Every line of a poem, she says, is a leap
and fall from heaven
to the next line

where, with renewed strength,
I say,
taking up the thought,
we face life's next terror, life's next wonder.

Covent Garden

J.M.W. Turner painted the violent sea—
boats tossed by storms at night, crews threatened
and battered by gales, masts breaking,
ships foundering. Night is torn by brushstrokes
of gold shining from a broken moon;
day is redeemed by light bursting forth
from a sun that blazes beyond the veil
of clouds and rain. Turner saw the world
as a dark place illumined by fire—
the Houses of Parliament burning to the ground,
the conflagration reflected in the Thames.
As Turner grew older, he painted dazzling skies
and brilliant sunsets, the very air aflame.
I've read that on his deathbed his last words
were "The sun is God." Or perhaps, "The son is God."
Either way, he was saying something about the light,
the sublime and supernatural light of heaven.
Turner's visions of stormy seas make one think
of Jesus in the midnight storm on the Sea of Galilee—
swamped boat sinking, the disciples dreading,
the gale shredding the sail, the wild wind, the deluge.
In the wave-tossed boat, Jesus rests, asleep on a pillow
while the rain falls harder and the night grows darker.
His disciples wake him and the Lord banishes the chaos
with the words: "Peace. Be Still." The sea calmed,
a clear, radiant light shows other boats saved on the water
and the light breaks like waves on the farther shore.

The Messengers

> Of making many books
> there is no end
>
> ECCLESIASTES

When they were little,
my children always needed "to talk"
and always what they had to say or ask
was "very, very important."
They missed me,
remote in the study,
devoted to the making of books.
They thought my devotion misplaced
and could leave me
to solitude
for brief moments only,
finding any number of excuses
to come into the room.
That's why
they had to interrupt
"one last time."
Seated,
I'd look into their eyes
as they stood by my desk,
perfectly still.
They'd take a breath
and search their minds;
for that which *is,*
is far off,
and deep, very deep;
who can find it out?
Endless questions burned,

a thousand fires they must extinguish—
How do birds fly?
Why are stars invisible
during the day?
Where does my shadow go
at night?
But just as often
they already had the answer—
ever surprising,
divine—
and which as messengers
they'd come to share with their father,
who laid down his pen,
took their hands,
and looking into their faces
listened
to each breathless soliloquy
describing and pondering
the sight of the eyes,
the light sweet,
their small voices
the miracle he was praying for
before they came into the room.

6

THE ITALIAN CANTOS

Love leads me on, from thought to thought,
from mountain to mountain, since every path blazed
proves opposed to the tranquil life.
If there is a stream or a fountain on a solitary slope,
if a shadowed valley lies between two hills,
the distressed soul calms itself there:
and, as Love invites it to,
now smiles, or weeps, or fears, or feels secure:
and my face that follows the soul where she leads
is turbid and then clear,
and remains only a short time in one mode:
so that a man expert in such a life would say
at the sight of me: "He is on fire, and uncertain of his state."

PETRARCH

Canto 1

Rome was sleeping.
Church domes shouldered the night sky.
Over Vatican Square, the statues of the saints
stood at rest. The piazzas were still.
Water trucks crept along, sweeping clean
the dusty streets, leaving glistening cobblestones.
And all night in the cavernous Termini,
I was waiting for the train, pacing the platform,
pacing as if I were writing,
searching for the best word, the right rhythm.
I was thinking of my wife, Laura,
Laura who was traveling alone in Venice without me.
She'd been staying in pensions,
but that night she'd taken a room at the Grand Hotel,
a rare extravagance for either of us,
and even at that moment she was sleeping.
I imagined her days in Venice—
sitting at one of the little tables on St. Mark's Square,
sipping a glass of white wine, taking it all in.
I liked to picture her
strolling through the galleries of the Accademia,
studying the mysterious shepherd
who guards and protects a woman and her nursing child
in the lightning-torn world of Giorgione's
La Tempesta. In my mind
I saw her wandering narrow lanes by still canals
or lingering in the crowds on the Bridge of Sighs
before returning to the hotel and retiring to her elegant bed,
where she'd turn the pages of her novel
and then, finally, close the book
and turn out the light.

Canto 2

"Listen," she said. "Hear me out.
The monastery is only a few dollars a day."
She put her tea down, that night last year,
and wiped some crumbs from the kitchen table.
"We can scrape up money for airfare," she said,
"and I can stay in pensions while you write."
I turned in my chair, away from her.
Looking back, I see that night I was afraid.
I looked around for an excuse to stay home,
but the tidy kitchen gave me no reason.
"Why a monastery?" I asked. "Why write there and not here?"
She didn't face me, as she usually did in such moments,
focusing more on the last crumb she'd missed
than on me, as if she were looking at something
I couldn't see. Then, treading lightly
to be sure that I heard her fully,
"Don't worry. I've thought this through.
I'll see Venice, and afterward we can meet,
you know, in that small town with the frescoes of…"
there went the last crumb between her fingertips,
flicked into the silver trash can by the white counter,
then turning, finally looking at me, "of Pinturicchio."
I looked at her blankly. Pinturicchio?
"In Spello—the little hill town in Umbria?
There's a chapel there, the Baglioni Chapel—
they call it Cappella Bella—'the beautiful chapel'—
with frescoes by Pinturicchio, 'the little painter,'
and we've never been there,
and I'd like to.
We should see the frescos.
We should see the frescos by Pinturicchio."

Canto 3

"And you'd go to Venice without me?" I said.
I hadn't realized it yet,
but she was being loving and purposeful.
"Richard, imagine seeing those frescoes."
She took a book from the bookshelf and read:
"No one thinks of Pinturicchio
in the same breath as Giotto or Fra Angelico,
but he's as true a painter as Raphael."
She'd done her research—
I saw she had bookmarked a dozen pages.
"So I would go off by myself?"
She swept her hand over the white counter,
searching for any last bread crumbs; there were none.
"Spello will be lovely. And we've never been.
And nearby—where is it?—maybe it's in Spoletto
or Assisi—there's another little chapel
with the most wonderful fresco.
Two angels in heaven hover over the risen Lord.
One removes the crown of thorns
while the other extends a crown of gold.
Imagine," she said. "Imagine—
such a great journey to make,
such a great distance
from *here* to that fading view of heaven."
Under the kitchen lights, my resistance wavered.
"So," Laura concluded, her eyes burning softer now,
satisfied, clapping her hands, settling the matter.
"You'll go to the monastery and I'll wait in Venice.
Then we'll meet in the piazza by the fountain in Spello
and visit the chapel and see the angels of paradise
crown Christ with the crown of glory."

Canto 4

The monastery's high walls, tower, chapel,
and cloister stones had been quarried from the mountain.
The light on the stones, their solidity and permanence,
made me believe the monastery had been blessed
and would endure forever,
though from the first day of my retreat that spring,
I saw how diligently the monks worked—
tending the chapel,
weeding and watering the vegetable gardens,
raking paths of crushed stone.
On my first morning I sat in the sun—
a sparrow alighting on a branch above me—
and saw a monk kneel with a pipe wrench
by a fountain where the water had stopped.
The monk's leathery face
and halo of wild white hair
reminded me of my friend Norby,
the carpenter I'd known longer than I'd been married,
the handyman who had helped me
rebuild three houses,
had taught me to measure twice,
to find the true level, and keep things plumb.
In broken Italian, I offered to help the monk.
He answered in precise English,
as if he had long ease with the language
and Americans like me. His name was Brother
Aloysius. "Al-o-*wish*-us," he corrected me, was born
in Rome of a Polish mother—like Apollinaire!—
and named after the patron saint of scholars and youths.
"And you are the poet staying with us,"
he said, rising, brushing off his heavy robe.

Canto 5

I lived in a monk's cell,
the solitude both dreadful and sweet.
Light from the cell's high window
fell on open notebooks.
At night, I poured myself out in written words;
mornings, I sat in silence
while the monks chanted psalms in the chapel.
During the long afternoons when the monks worked—
never idle, always selfless, mindful of devotions—
I studied sonnets in the cloistered garden,
a twig of rosemary plucked from the courtyard
fragrant between my fingers.
And again at night I'd write in my notebooks,
pace the cell, endure the slow and empty hours;
or seeking visions that never came,
I'd lie on the narrow bed
like a man hidden in the cleft of a rock,
listening for the voice out of the whirlwind.
And while hidden in the monastery,
I wondered whether my wife in Venice was thinking about me.
Lying in bed with my head on the tiny pillow,
I saw her, maybe a little sad when it rained
as she walked along the Zattere,
but happy to buy gifts for the children—
a Pinocchio marionette for Sarah,
carnival masks for the boys.
I saw her window-shopping for lace and glass
and hoped she'd buy something for herself before
stopping in a pastry shop to sip tea and write postcards,
just as attentive to the crumbs of Venice
as to the crumbs in our kitchen.

Canto 6

In the refectory, the monks ate simple meals. Then,
after one of the younger brothers had read aloud in Latin,
they would all intone a prayer and rise at once
and disappear down the halls to perform duties
unknown and mysterious to me. One night,
sitting alone at the long wooden table—
my empty plate cleared away, my stomach still hungry—
I thought of home
and cooking big suppers for my children
on those nights Laura worked late.
I recalled helping with math homework, piano,
enforcing the evening's ablutions,
then reading to the children until bedtime,
stories about love and sacrifice and honor.
I wanted the story of my children's lives
to be filled with courage and love
and to be full of grace,
unlike the days of my childhood.
As a boy I knew desperate nights.
I'd end up out the back door,
down the porch steps, the screen door banging.
I'd stand in the dark yard, looking
at the dark boughs of the magnolia,
the branches overhead, their strong arms,
arms that could hold you, lift you up,
arms that wouldn't bend or break.
I didn't know what I was looking for
there in the swaying branches overhead
as my boyhood heartache and unhappiness
mingled with the sweet perfume
of the tree's white blossoms.

Canto 7

Sitting at the refectory's long wooden table
after the evening meal, I remembered
as a boy I wanted to sit down with my father
and discuss deep things with him, *life...*
But men of his time had a code.
My father's code was to talk about the weather.
"How's your weather?" he'd say.
If I wanted to talk about some weighty matter,
something important,
he'd listen quietly and patiently and then he'd say,
"Let me tell you about the weather."
My father would turn the conversation
to clear skies, or cloudy and storms,
as if that were the most important thing on earth.
He'd talk about his flying days during the War,
about thunderclouds, wind-driven rain,
blizzards, sandstorms, lightning,
ice on the wings. He said
weather was a matter of life and death.
I remembered calling long-distance one night,
seeking his solace and comfort,
wanting him to tell me how to live.
My father waited for me to finish what I was saying,
then eagerly told me about the terrible
thunderstorm, asking whether I could hear
the rain beating down. Suddenly,
neither of us was talking.
I stood with the phone to my ear,
listening to drumming on the skylight
in my parents' kitchen, picturing an old man
holding the receiver up to the thunder and darkness.

Canto 8

It was the hour before compline.
I lingered at the fellowship table
while the monks said their evening prayers.
I thought about my father, all the things
he'd seen and done that I had not.
In the War he logged over a million miles.
He flew over the Himalayas
and the jungles of Burma,
survived
one hundred eighty-nine missions.
Sitting at the empty table in the refectory,
I gazed out the window at the violet night,
the darkness. Outside,
the mountain was quiet,
but I could still hear the thunder
and rattle of rain on my parents' skylight
and see him,
an old soldier who endured,
his frail arm raised in the darkness.
A lifetime later, a father now with my own home,
I pictured tucking in his grandchildren,
kissing them good night, turning out the lights,
then lingering in the doorway,
my heart wordless in the peaceful dark.
The night-light's carousel spinning
and casting silhouettes
of horses prancing on the ceiling and walls,
I'd think of the miles I'd come,
sitting next to Sarah on the piano bench
or across the dinner table from William and Andrew,
talking about the weather.

Canto 9

The next day in the stables,
Aloysius spread hay with a pitchfork
and fed two mules named Giacomo and Giovanni.
The monk inquired about my work, my "*poesia.*"
I shrugged, twirling a piece of straw,
a pen without ink,
before tossing the straw on the ground.
"I'm struggling," I confessed,
"with poems I've tried a thousand times to write
but never get a handle on."
"Such as?"
"Well, there's a memory
of my mother—her loneliness."
Aloysius raised his eyebrows, urging me on.
"I'm young—twelve, thirteen. It's late autumn.
The days are cold and short; night comes early.
Evening bells ring out at six o'clock,
and I walk home in the dark from the playground,
and I can hear the dry leaves crackling under my feet.
I find my mother in the kitchen, ironing shirts—
my father's white oxfords.
The windows are black with night
and dinner's warm on the stove.
The aroma of roasting potatoes
makes me realize I'm hungry.
The table's laid and waiting—
the china plates edged with blue and pink flowers—
and she's got, on all the kitchen cupboard knobs,
a dozen white shirts hanging silent as ghosts."
In their stalls, James and John munched hay,
blinking their big mule eyes as if pondering the long-ago scene.

Canto 10

"That sounds like a portrait of love,"
Aloysius said, lifting a sloshing wooden bucket
and pouring fresh water into the mules' trough.
"A mother's love—cooking, ironing shirts."
He nodded approvingly. The mules drank. I went on.
"The thing is, my mother was deaf."
And then—to clarify what "deaf" means—
"She couldn't hear me."
I stood silent to let this cold fact punctuate
the sweet, thick, hay-scented air of the barn.
"When I was little," I continued, "my mother
would hold my face in her hands—like a book—
and read my lips to hear me."
"A poem *is* eternity's vessel," the monk said with a sly smile.
"Yes, yes, I know," I said, "but in this poem,
I drop my bag and my mother doesn't look up—
she never did—she just keeps on ironing. *Ironing*,"
I repeated, adding, "She was so sad, so lonely..."
Aloysius said nothing. I stumbled. "The problem...
in the poem, I mean... I never find the words...
so close to my mother, unseen, unheard."
Aloysius put down his bucket, picked up his pitchfork,
and turned to face me. He had finished his chores.
"You are saying that you felt like a ghost?" he said.
"Well, yes," I said. "A ghost. I always felt like a ghost."
Aloysius stood his pitchfork on end, the iron tines raised high.
"No," the monk said, shaking his head. "You were no ghost.
And you did not see your mother's loneliness. No.
If you had seen her loneliness, you would have spoken—
you would have kissed the dear woman. But you said nothing.
Because what you saw as a child was your own loneliness."

Canto 11

That night I lay on my side in the dark,
interrogating the wall
about sadness and loneliness.
The wall answered with memories
of my five-year-old nephew,
who drowned in the river
behind my sister's house.
Once when I was visiting,
he had come home from kindergarten
and called out, "Uncle Richard!"
Later in his room—
a room as small as the one
in which I was now talking to the wall—
he taught me a funny dance,
his little body walking backward
as Michael Jackson played on the stereo.
"Moonwalking," he called it.
Later that evening we threw bread on the water
for the ducks he loved.
We made little paper boats
and watched them float out with the tide
as it got dark, and the river and night
became one. A few weeks later,
one evening when I was home alone
in the farmhouse in the mountains,
I answered the telephone.
It was my father's voice:
our beloved boy had drowned in the river.
In my cell in the dark
the wall asked,
"*Are you beginning to see?*"

Canto 12

My sister's house in Virginia is built of stone
from granite quarried in Scotland
and shipped to America in the late 1800s
to raise a church that was never built.
The stone house now a century old,
the river ever peaceful,
my sister lives there still
and every new morning from her kitchen window
she looks out on the water where her child drowned,
the surface still as glass or shirred by wind.
The tides come and go each day,
and though it is said no one enters the same river twice,
lying in my cell, the wall vivid, I could see again
the policeman, the red lights, the television crew,
the strangers with flashlights searching the yard,
searching everywhere, the garage, the cars, the trunks,
even making older brother Thomas
open all the boxes in the house,
as if his little brother were simply hiding in one.
The divers found the body underwater,
just a few feet from the tree
with the high branch and the tire swing he loved.
My sister told me she stood in her yard that night
and all the bushes burned.
She told me she lifted her hands to God
and God cut off her hands;
she fell to her knees and God cut her legs off.
When I was leaving for Italy I stopped to see my sister.
We stood by the tidal river behind her house.
Such love. I told her I'd never known such love.
"Now," she said, "all the world is holy ground."

Canto 13

Walking the stone path in the garden,
I told Aloysius that as a boy
I often stood at gravesides,
saying goodbye to aunts and uncles
who died in ways a child could never have foreseen:
Aunt Opal's car somehow stalled on the tracks
and was hit by a speeding train;
Uncle Brown fell from a tree and broke his neck;
Aunt Jean, for whom my sister, Jean Sheldon, is named,
returned to dust and ash
one night when her house burned down.
"'The days run away,'" I said
"'like wild horses over the hills.'"
Aloysius looked at me with sudden sympathy.
"Ah, the poet speaks," he said.
"Oh," I said, "that wasn't me.
That was Bukowski. An American poet."
Aloysius smiled. "That's a good line."
"Poets are always remembering
other poets' lines," I said.
Aloysius looked skyward and closed his eyes;
and he hesitated a moment,
making sure he got each word right.
Then he looked at me.
"A poet also said,
'Eternity is in love
with the productions of time.'"
We stood there, pondering our wisdom.
Then he clapped his hands and said,
"And right now it is time for me to be peeling potatoes
and for you to be at your desk, writing."

Canto 14

Aloysius had said *Look at the world—*
that a poet must look through his eyes
and tell the truth about what he sees.
Writing in my cell—
time unreal, the mind on fire—
I paced and opened books
and stood on tiptoe at the high window,
looking out at the green valley.
At the table I had begun writing
the poem about my mother.
I lifted the page and putting on my glasses
saw the old lines I'd written
about the evening bells and the kitchen
with its bright lights and night-black windows
where my mother stood ironing.
But now I changed the ending,
finding the right words by looking and seeing
and writing what really happened…
I come in from the cold to the foyer
and drop my bag of books.
My mother, ironing, does not hear.
I linger unseen in the kitchen doorway.
My mother, who thinks she is alone, is singing.
"…Teach me some melodious sonnet,
Sung by flaming tongues above.
Praise the mount! I'm fixed upon it,
Mount of Thy redeeming love."
I listen and wait
and when she falls quiet,
I move toward her and touch her on the shoulder
with my autumn-chilled hand.

Canto 15

I reread the last line,
decided to cut "autumn-chilled,"
but couldn't seem to find a simpler adjective.
I went to the window again,
stood on tiptoe and looked out.
Nothing came to me:
the adjectives had all been taken.
I returned to the table and rearranged the line.
I move toward her and reach out
and touch her on the shoulder.
Still not there.
I decided to leave it for another time,
but with the image of Aloysius peeling potatoes
so fresh in my mind,
I kept at it.
I move toward her and reach out
and touch her on the shoulder
and my mother looks up,
takes my autumn-chilled hand in hers,
and says my name.
Better.
I took a victory lap around the room,
then came back to the poem.
A voice in my head said, "Richard,
you still have to cut 'autumn-chilled.'"
So I gave "autumn-chilled" to Bukowski,
who, somewhere in eternity,
may find it useful for one of his own poems.
My mother looks up,
takes my hand in hers,
and says my name.

Canto 16

On my last night in the monastery,
a storm ravaged the mountain.
Lightning cleaved the darkness,
leaving the night in ruins.
In terrible flashes of light,
I saw the cell without me in it—
an empty bed,
an empty desk.
As a savage rain grew gentle,
I lay on the bed, listening
until deep in the night
the storm abated and stillness came, quiet.
In the morning I saw the bright morning star,
always so low on the horizon.
And there, those shafts of dawn light—
had someone taken them directly
from one of those medieval paintings?
I looked again to make sure they were real.
When I heard the monks chanting matins,
I knew it was time to leave. I imagined
Laura at the promised fountain in the sun—
her head tilted back, the sun on her pale skin—
dipping her hand in the water to cool her neck,
loose strands of her hair damp against her shoulders.
Right now in the Grand Hotel, I thought,
she would be waking in her bed, refreshed,
her thoughts serene, and hoping the same for me
as I stood in my spartan cell,
thunderstruck
at the tiny
window.

Canto 17

That rain-refreshed morning,
I left my bag at the door of the empty cell,
but took my poems with me—
a bundle of pages tied with string—
for one last visit to the chapel
before going to Rome to catch the train
to the little town where I would meet Laura.
I walked the stone path through the garden—
the summer vegetables already tall, lush—
detouring to take one last labyrinth walk
around the rosemary hedge in the courtyard
to the little fountain in the center.
I had come here every day during my visit.
I would splash my face with the water.
Today the water was warm.
That first day in spring
the water was cold, almost icy.
I put my poems down on the path
and cupped the water with both hands—
a clear lens showing the lines in my palm.
I looked up at the chapel,
which this morning seemed smaller,
no more important than a gardener's shack.
Running my fingers along the tips of the rosemary hedge,
poems under my arm,
I retraced my steps in the circle
and for the first time counted each step.
"Forty steps," I thought, "who would have believed it?"
"Forty steps," I said aloud,
as if speaking made it so,
as if speaking anything makes it so.

Canto 18

A monk had just left the chapel
before I stepped from the light
and over the high wooden threshold
into the tenebrous place of worship.
I kept my gaze on the floor
as my eyes adjusted
to the dimness of the chapel,
lighted only by a few votive candles.
The floor stones echoed
as I walked toward the altar.
The chapel's silence,
its mellow acoustic calm,
was a welcome balm,
heaven sent.
I lit a candle,
then moved into a pew and sat listening.
I had come to the end—
not only of my retreat, but of something more.
I remembered Thomas Aquinas
at the end of his life.
Work still to be done on the unfinished *Summa*,
but his pen lay silent.
His young secretary
urged him to keep writing
but the old man said that his words
and all his writing
and all his books
seemed like "straw"
compared to those things
that he had now seen
and that had been revealed to him.

Canto 19

Sitting in the chapel, I undid my bundle of poems
and read the first few titles—
"White Shirts," "The River Ever Peaceful,"
"All the World Is Holy Ground,"
"The Pitchfork," "What the Wall Said"…
I thought how much it meant to me
to write them, the gift,
then stacked all the pages once more,
tied the string tighter, and sat a moment longer,
my mind at rest,
the stone font and holy water beside me,
the only sound the soft guttering of the votive candles.
Thomas died expounding on the Song of Songs
and said that though we can't do the work
of angels, we can at least write of them.
All the angels. Laura. My father. Aloysius.
I considered all the books I'd read
and all the books in the monks' library.
They all said different things
but they all said the same thing,
a truth paradoxical and inscrutable
that burns within us like a fire.
I walked down the aisle to the altar
and placed the bundle of poems there,
the only thing I had to offer,
the lightest thing I'd done in months.
"Straw for the fire," I said.
That, and so much more, now understood.
Then I walked out of the chapel,
stepping over the door's high threshold,
back into my life.

Canto 20

My clothes smelled of incense
when Brother Aloysius drove me down the mountain
in the monastery's small white van.
The road was narrow, one blind curve after another,
but Aloysius knew the way and drove
by faith. One hand resting on the wheel,
he turned and asked about my poetry
and what I had written in my cell.
His smile disarmed me; I shook my head
and shrugged my shoulders, not knowing what to say.
He said, "No, no, it is important.
The writing in poetry isn't like the writing in newspapers.
We still need prophets—don't you agree?"
We were crossing a bridge
at the bottom of the mountain.
Before I could think of an answer,
before I knew how I felt,
we had reached the other side.
Soon we were in Rome,
where beside the white van
on a busy street near the Spanish Steps,
he put his hand on my shoulder and prayed for me.
Then he gave me a gift wrapped in butcher paper—
a red, calfskin writing notebook.
"For your poems," he said.
I flipped through the empty pages and looked at him.
"We all must live," he said.
The sun was behind him,
the light in my eyes when he said,
"We're all made of dust and glory.
And that's what you must write about."

Canto 21

At the Spanish Steps near Keats's house,
I stood outside a restaurant where years earlier
Laura and I had dined the year we were married.
Under an arbor of grapevines and bougainvillea
we had talked about the room where Keats died.
Laura talked about the brevity of life, about friendship,
how Severn stayed with his friend to the end.
While the waiters would come and go—
dazzling me with delicious trays of cheese and figs,
bowls of pasta with sea urchin and swordfish caviar,
or garlic-laced snails in their black shells—
Laura wondered aloud how death
never made life meaningless for Keats,
but all was truth and beauty.
She loved how he loved Fanny Brawne,
and there in the restaurant,
she held her hand out over the white tablecloth
and quoted from memory,
"This living hand, now warm and capable
of earnest grasping, would, if it were cold
and in the icy silence of the tomb,
so haunt thy days and chill thy dreaming nights that"
—the waiter poured water, listened, walked away—
"that thou wouldst wish thine own heart dry of blood
so in my veins red life might stream again,
and thou be conscience-calm'd—see here it is—
I hold it towards you." As twilight fell,
I remembered our laughter and realized
it would be too sad to dine without Laura, alone.
I bought a lemon *granita*, hoisted my rucksack,
and made my way on foot to the train station.

Canto 22

And so, late that night,
I found myself pacing in the station,
the grand lobby empty, one or two trains
silent and dark on the sidings.
Midnight had passed with memories
of the monastery and Brother Aloysius,
who like Saint Francis praised everything—
sun and moon, the little flowers.
Now somewhere the train, my train,
the train that would reunite me with my wife,
was speeding over the land toward Rome.
I walked to the end of the long, gray platform
then turned and walked back to the station
where there was nothing to do,
only stand and wait.
The arrivals board was quiet. My watch said 4 a.m.
The plan was to meet Laura in Spello
at a fountain near the chapel at noon.
Eight hours. An eternity.
I sat on a bench and shrugged off my rucksack.
Inside I found the book my wife had given me,
a volume of Petrarch's poems,
along with my Bible and passport.
And wrapped in butcher paper,
the new red notebook, all those pages to fill.
I thought how others know us
better than we know ourselves, our needs—
my wife, who saw through my confusion
and sent me away to write,
and Aloysius, who said to fill the notebook
with dust and glory.

Canto 23

I unwrapped the butcher paper
and ran my hand over the notebook's cover,
the color of blood and royalty.
In recent years all my notebooks had been black.
Hemingway wrote in blue-backed notebooks,
the color of sky and water.
He'd look out over the roofs of Paris
and think, "Do not worry."
He'd tell himself that all he had to do was
"write one true sentence."
Sitting here on a cold bench
in the middle of the night in Rome,
what would I write? Perhaps
I would begin again with a love poem,
a simple little love poem.
I would write, as Aloysius had asked me to,
a poem for Laura, knowing
that a poem dedicated to Laura
is a poem for the world.
It's always been that way.
I stood and looked down the tracks,
the lines that reached into the night's darkness,
and taking stock, I found how deeply
I believe in the power of words to bless.
Write one true sentence.
I thought of Laura, walking
past brilliant palaces in the night.
I imagined her in the Grand Hotel, dreaming,
and considered: could true art ever be
something other than the act of love,
love for one other, love for the world?

Canto 24

Attenzione! Was that Laura calling to me?
Was dawn announcing its approach?
Attenzione! Ah, a voice on the loudspeaker.
I took off my glasses and rubbed my eyes,
then put my glasses on again
and searched the empty tracks.
I turned the other way and saw approaching
a pregnant girl, smiling at me, because,
I realized, I was smiling, laughing at myself.
The first person to join me on the platform,
she stood waiting quietly by herself.
Overhead, the departure board
tumbled its white letters and numbers,
revealing the myriad and ever-changing destinations
in which a man might place his hope—
Perugia, Siracusa, Abruzzo,
Milan, Naples, Siena, Pisa, and Florence,
Positano and Portofino, Verona, Asolo,
Ravello, Orvieto.
The world turned on its axis.
The train was coming,
speeding through black mountain tunnels
and slipping past terraced vineyards under the moon.
The entire universe must be spinning,
I thought, the stars and planets swirling in dizzy orbits.
People now were filling the concourse,
milling about, Italians with rolling cases,
day-trippers with backpacks,
young couples accompanied by small children—
the ever-beginning world, a new day.
Attenzione! Attenzione!

Canto 25

I caught myself staring at the young woman—
she seemed to step right out of a painting
by Vermeer. I thought of Holland,
the canals and the houseboats
with their flowerpot gardens.
Her eyes were the blue
of the delft vase
I bought my mother
on my first trip to Europe,
and when the young woman's eyes met mine,
I said hello in Italian, "*Buon giorno.*"
She looked up,
shyly,
the globe of her belly
in her hands like a mystery.
When she said nothing in reply,
I fumbled for something
to say in Dutch,
and blurted out,
"*Lang niet gezien*"—
long time, no see.
The girl blushed and turned away.
I bowed to inscrutability,
then turned at the sound
of a distant whistle,
and leaning forward
looked down the tracks,
where, in the farthest darkness,
there appeared
a small
light.

Canto 26

The engine rolled past, towering high,
coasting along the platform,
its grand carriage of brightly lighted coaches slowing,
red-curtained sleeping cars
receding down the rail into the last vestiges of night.
The pregnant girl, suitcase at her feet, waited,
as with the dying sound of distant thunder,
the train came to a stop.
The girl's face remained serene,
as if the master really had painted her.
I wondered what my face revealed.
Could the girl beside me see I was a traveler,
ready to board and travel the unknown road?
Passengers emerged, spilling from the cars,
weary and disheveled—
a girl with long hair tousled and lovely from sleep,
an unshaven old man in a rumpled gray suit
held together by black suspenders.
Bleary-eyed and walking stiffly, all looked about,
as if they'd landed on some alien shore.
A lone soldier—
crisp shirt, creased pants, polished buttons—
hoisted a duffel on his shoulder
and led the way. Soon all the travelers
busied and burdened themselves with heavy bags
and rolling carts and suitcases,
and began their exodus down the platform
toward the station, a host of Romans
staggering past, as if the train, which had carried them
safely through the wilderness of night,
were a moving kingdom and they had now come home.

Canto 27

The train stole through Rome.
Resting by the window, I remembered
sitting at the table with tea, home in America,
a book of paintings open between us,
the house cloistered by a night of snow.
Laura had leaned close and I could feel
her warmth when she told me
we *would* see the frescoes.
She turned the pages and
touched her finger to the book's
illustration of an angel hovering
over the Lord's wounded head
and removing the crown of thorns
and putting on the crown of paradise.
We rolled past Rome's outskirts.
Beyond the window, I could see
cypresses on hills and farmhouses waking.
I closed my eyes and tried to sleep,
but the train kept stopping
to let people off, to let people on.
At one of the stops,
when I was half dreaming,
I sensed someone sit beside me.
I allowed one lid to open—
awake with one eye, asleep with the other—
and glimpsed the face of a man
who worked in the sun,
a man my age, bearded, heavy.
I closed my eye and moved back into the dream.
A few minutes later,
I heard the conductor ask for his ticket.

Canto 28

In the years before I met Laura, I remember
riding night trains from Paris to Rome,
Rome to Palermo, the train passing by towns so small
they seemed no more real than wishes
a man might make to be healed.
As my heavyset friend dreamed and snored next to me,
I looked out the window, a little sleepy and dreamy myself,
and thought how the wish Laura made back in our kitchen
will be fulfilled today. We'll stand together
in the chapel and gaze at Pinturicchio's paintings
and by that vision be renewed.
Now I realize this was always her plan.
And when the day ends, arm in arm
like Italians we'll enjoy the *passeggiata,*
that slow stroll through town at twilight,
stopping at one *stuzzichini* bar after another,
sitting at the tables, drinking wine
and sharing little snacks. And later
in the hotel room bed, how, I wondered,
shall we sleep, being so happy?
We'll turn out the lamp and undress in the dark,
a little shy with each other,
though we'll leave the balcony doors open
to the sound of laughter rising
and the revving of the ubiquitous scooters
with the young boy and girl holding tight
as they race in the street below.
Such were my thoughts as the train sped north
and the day brightened and the train slowed
and stopped at a station at the foot of the mountains,
at Spello.

Canto 29

The purple seat beside me was empty.
I must have fallen asleep
and the bearded man must have gotten off
at some little town full of wishes.
I strapped on my bag and disembarked,
nodding to Spello's blue-capped porters
disappointed to see me with only a rucksack.
I stood in the morning light
in the tiny, unhurried station.
Perhaps the porters could see before them a man
who carried only the lightness of victory,
a man who rubbed his chest, his heart,
as the station windows filled with sun,
the air with the music of human voices.
I remembered Aloysius one day in the garden
hanging the brothers' washed clothes to dry.
I was telling him I felt lost and wasted,
that I was like parched ground.
Art had always been my guide through life,
leading me through inward mazes,
but the monk told me simply to go into my cell,
and that my cell would tell me everything—
that too much striving, too much introspection,
takes you away from God and the world,
and leaves a man waterless and wandering.
So like a wise and prudent monk, I stopped
at a newsstand and bought a bottle of water
and a city map of Spello.
The fleeting world before me now like the sweetest gift,
I stepped from the station into the street outside,
and said to myself, "To the fountain."

Canto 30

Outside Spello's city gate,
I looked at my watch—8:30—
and with my fingertip tapped the watch face
to hurry time forward.
Laura would not arrive for hours.
I entered a coffee bar
and ordered a cappuccino.
For the next two hours, I talked
to anyone drinking beside me,
switching from cappuccino to espresso.
Sensing fellow pilgrims and spiritual comrades,
I spoke with a dozen Italians
lingering and drinking coffee,
workingmen with muddy boots.
Though none spoke English,
I said, "A poem is nothing,"
and waited for a response.
The workers looked at me.
Coffee stimulates the poppy seeds in the brain.
I might be a tourist,
but they were good-hearted and listened.
I pressed on.
From my pocket I pulled out my pen,
pointing the pen like a maestro's baton
to punctuate and stress each word.
"A poem is nothing
if not a sign
pointing to the holy
hidden from our eyes."
The workers nodded;
I knew they knew I was on to something.

Canto 31

"To Italia!" I said and held up my cup,
a toast to Italy's broken and headless statues.
The workers nodded in agreement,
understanding everything,
talking among themselves now
about Dante, I assumed,
for they were Italians
and their great subject was love.
My speech over, my *ars poetica* complete,
I put the last empty cup down
and reached for my wallet,
but the barista said my bill had been paid—
an act of grace, who knows by whom?
Fortified with caffeine—
two cappuccinos and three espressos—
I set out on my journey,
the workers tipping their dirty caps
and waving through the café window
that was misted from the churning
and chugging espresso machine.
On the street, taxi drivers
stood at attention as I approached.
But I had decided to walk
the steep cobblestone streets,
to climb the mountain on my own.
Beneath the Porta Consolare, I looked up
at the statues of the family above the arch.
The woman there resembled my Laura.
Inside the old town's high walls
I opened and unfolded the map
and saw the Cappella Bella marked in red.

Canto 32

What was the right word
to describe the morning's peace
on the narrow lanes of ancient stone?
What words
describe the feeling
that one is seeing the morning's beauty anew,
as if for the first time,
the world,
incarnate,
in that miraculous moment?
In the dark-shadowed passageways
I welcomed the companionship
whenever a red or blue door opened
and a solitary soul
stepped lightly onto the stones
to walk with me,
the American tourist,
climbing the town's streets.
The opened doors revealed
still-quiet courtyards,
patio gardens with oleander and lemon trees,
motorbikes and bicycles,
tables and chairs,
windows with lace curtains.
On a high iron balcony
a woman in a white silk robe
watering her flowerpots
stopped and stood,
her head raised, looking at the sky.
I stopped and looked up, also,
and saw the sky was beautiful.

Canto 33

As I was staring at the sky,
three nuns rushed past, startling me.
Their long habits rustled up the hill,
their rosaries swinging
and clacking from their woolen belts.
Their black shoes clicked on the stones,
and the nuns vanished around the corner.
They climbed so effortlessly,
I stood aside to let them pass,
but also to catch my breath.
I leaned against a wall.
My old legs ached.
My lungs burned
and my heart seemed ready to burst.
In some *fondo del sacco* of my mind,
the thought actually occurred to me
that an American poet,
unused to these steep streets,
which the old people of Spello climb every day,
could die in this place
trying to reach the fountain to meet his wife.
I saw a hand writing my name on the fountain's pool,
but it didn't matter; I would live
like the nuns or Aloysius,
in my own form of the day-to-day,
seeing heaven in a glass of water.
I thought of my poems on the altar
and wondered whether Brother Aloysius
had found them
and used them to feed the fire
in the monastery's kitchen.

Canto 34

Higher up the mountain, bells were ringing,
and farther up the lane children,
free from school for the summer
and liberated from their heavy book-bags,
ran laughing and shouting, light as birds.
The stone wall cool against my back,
I took long, slow, deep breaths,
and to calm myself thought again of my wife,
who with her insights and knowledge of me
insisted I make this trip, begin this journey,
back when I was pacing the house
and she knew there was healing
to be done among chapels with God-infused paintings
and ancient Roman temples, shrines and ruins,
marble and stone warmed in the sun.
At a flower stall the vendor's metal buckets
overflowed with colorful blooms—
asters, cosmos, daisies, roses, oleanders, and lilies.
I pictured Laura and imagined the chapel,
realizing that today was the day we would see
the paintings of "the little painter,"
Pinturicchio,
and I would sit in the church
holding Laura's hand.
I climbed again, now with quick steps,
felt the narrow street under my feet
almost imperceptibly widen,
the steeply pitched lane grow level,
as before me in the town square
the fountain Laura had prophesied
blazed in the morning light.

Canto 35

As I rested in the sunny square,
a gust of swallows swept the sky
and disappeared behind tiled rooftops,
a line of poetry no one could ever write.
My wife would arrive at noon
at the very fountain she had chosen.
Even now, I thought, her train
must be crossing the valley,
arriving at the station.
She'll not climb the town's steep streets
like her foolish husband.
She'll tip a porter to carry her bags.
And to ascend the mountain,
she'll be sensible.
She won't risk her heart.
She'll hire a taxi, its horn beeping
before every treacherous corner.
As church bells ring,
she'll sit in the backseat,
look through her dark glasses
and wave through the open window
at the children, smiling because
she is happy, because she, too,
sees the swallows soaring.
Laura would arrive punctually,
precisely at noon,
just when the bells tolled;
I also knew she would appear
suddenly, unexpectedly,
as love often does,
and call my name across the square.

Canto 36

So under a sky from bygone days,
a clear sky Bellini
or Mantegna might have painted,
and beside me the fragrant bouquet,
splayed on the fountain's stone rim,
I uncapped my black fountain pen
in search of one true sentence.
I opened the red notebook,
and wrote this poem
for Laura:
I love you because
you love riding trains—
looking out the window
at fields of sunflowers—
and are glad to stay a few nights
at the Grand Hotel in Venice
and ride in sleek gondolas,
serenaded by handsome men,
but now the time has come
and I'm here at the fountain
waiting for you to join me—
waiting for you to show me,
as noonday bells ring for joy,
the chapel with the frescoes by
Pinturicchio, the little painter;
so come quickly, find me
resting on sun-warmed stone,
face freshly washed, eyes closed,
my mouth almost smiling,
the book of poems you gave me
open in my hands.

Canto 37

Closing my notebook,
capping my pen,
and putting away my rucksack,
I closed my eyes. The day was so bright
the darkness behind my eyelids was golden,
and in the golden light behind my eyes,
I saw I was a grape in a winepress
or dough in the strong hands of a baker.
I was sorrow transformed into joy,
and I would sing about this life
I share with street sweepers
and train conductors and pregnant girls
who only want to go home to Holland
just as Laura and I will soon want to go home
to America and our children, whose lives
are countries as beautiful as Italy,
as Rome and Venice and Spello.
I leaned back against the fountain,
envisioning my wife in her white dress,
her cadenced and metrical walk,
her hands keeping tempo,
the elision of her shadow keeping measure,
the dark figure gliding across
the square's sun-splashed stones
and saying my name.
Then, in the sun by the fountain,
I fell asleep and continued the dream:
I saw Laura on the train.
She was looking out the window,
thinking to herself, her voice a song,
and I could hear her innermost thoughts.

Canto 38

Fields of sunflowers
drift past the train's window
as Laura daydreams, already reminiscing
about her one extravagant night at the Grand Hotel,
happy to have ridden in sleek black gondolas,
serenaded by handsome men.
She wonders, would her husband
have enjoyed Venice, too—
the cozy pensions, the silken water?
I wish he would let himself be happy…
as when he looks up and sees the swallows—
I wish he'd let his heart soar.
On a distant hill, Spello shines golden.
She finds her sunglasses
and exits the station with porters who carry her bags.
She asks the boy leaning against his taxi
to take her up the mountain,
trusting this child
who beeps his horn at every corner
to get her from the outskirts of town
to the mountaintop alive. In the taxi,
she looks back across the green valley,
thinking how far she has traveled,
the years. She wonders and hopes
that the time in the monastery
has been good, that her husband
was happy writing, content and at peace.
She'll ask, and when he says
Yes, as she hopes he will,
she'll ask has he written something
for her, a few lines, simple and pure.

Canto 39

The taxi takes
terraced switchback
roads that, like a miracle,
climb and circle back
to drop her at a small hotel
a little higher up the mountain
than the square and the fountain
where her husband is waiting.
The hotel is perfect—
quiet and down-to-earth,
the room simple and unassuming,
the bed white,
the balcony open to the sky.
She leaves her bags,
heavy with the gifts
she will take home to the children,
and carrying nothing,
walks downhill toward the square,
feeling free and light.
She says hello to the grocer,
gives the street sweeper a smile,
and nods at three nuns
who lovingly watch the schoolchildren
running wild through the square.
In her hand,
two coins are ready,
American pennies brought from home
so she and her husband can wish as one
and toss them in the fountain,
but looking about
she doesn't see him, her husband, anywhere.

Canto 40

Then above the square, bells ring out.
The bells ring and ring for joy,
but her heart sinks:
where is he? She doesn't find him
until she walks a few steps farther,
circling around the fountain
to find him on the other side,
sitting alone, leaning back against the stone,
his eyes closed, almost smiling,
a book of poems in his lap,
sleeping, it seems, and dreaming,
a bouquet of flowers
on the ground beside him.
Spray from the fountain
dazzles and sparkles in the sunlight.
She looks around the square:
the nuns and the children have vanished.
There's no one around.
The square is empty, save the two of them.
She steps closer, then stops.
She takes off her sunglasses.
Never, she thinks,
have I seen my husband more peaceful.
She hesitates for a moment, thinking—
as swallows cross the sky
and the last bell echoes in the distance—
that it seems a shame to wake him.
But she does. She comes close,
and kneeling beside him,
she takes his hand
and says his name.

7

ALL THE TIME IN THE WORLD

one moment the life inside you is a stone,
and the next,
a star

RAINER MARIA RILKE

Goodbye

My aged and infirm father's health
faded over the course of three years,
so that when I'd fly to Virginia Beach
to see him in the house by the ocean,

I had occasion at the end of each visit—
knowing each visit could be the *last*—
to repeat my final farewells yet again.
In the sunroom I would take his hand

and tell him things I had never said.
He would slightly shake his head *no*
when I confessed I was not a good son,
that I was sorry, but would lie quietly

when I tried to express the depth
of my gratitude. For my father was
a good father to me, and at the end
I was able to look him in the eye

and thank him for all he had taught me.
Our last visits were surprisingly happy.
I'd said all my heart could think to say,
and we were free to enjoy the light

pouring warm through the windows,
to luxuriate in the sweet slowness of time.
I think that was his final gift to me,
his comfort with time and silence,

and I was reminded of days when
under the hanging lamp at the kitchen table

he and I built model airplanes.
We'd unfold the directions and lay out

all the interrelated parts I found
so difficult to understand or deal with,
and with perfect equanimity he'd explain—
in clear terms a boy could understand—

how the jet engine fit together,
or the aerodynamics of a riveted iron wing.
But mostly we worked in silence,
my father advising to go slow

and think things through,
then fit each piece together exactly,
telling me, sitting beside him, never to rush—
we had all the time in the world.

Unwritten Excerpt from My Daughter's Diary: "The Hollow Men" and My Father

I rejoice that things are as they are

T.S. ELIOT

My father sees affirmations in the saddest lives
and the most sorrowful poetry.
All afternoon in a London pub,
he nurses a pint of bitter
and reads Eliot. Poetry, he says,
widens his ken
and affords a clear vision
of the interconnectedness of all things.
He says "The Hollow Men" makes him think
of poor Vivienne Eliot, the poet's delicate wife
who suffered nervous breakdowns.
My once-unbelieving father now stands,
against the odds, like Eliot,
on the strong rock of faith,
but it is Vivienne's fragility and self-absorption
my father relates to, having had in his youth
his own trembling chapters.
Brilliant but mad Vivienne: divorced, abandoned,
and left to die in a mental institution.
He sighs; hollow men
do not know how to love, he says.
My father's eyes are blue; in them I see no judgment.
The world is fallen, he says, as he lifts his glass
but does not drink. Even the poets are lost, he says.
And so how to account for the pleasure
Eliot's poems give my father?
How do I account for the joy

my father finds in each moment,
his loving attention to the smallest details?
Everything, in his mind, deserves affirmation,
even brokenness, even the wasteland,
believing all will be redeemed.
He finally smiles at me and tells me
he counts his blessings.
He asks whether I like my tea,
am I enjoying my cookie,
what am I writing about in my notebook.
In order I answer: *yes,* and *it's delicious,* and *nothing.*
He smiles again: he knows when I say "nothing"
it is secret code for "I'm writing
about everything in the universe.
I'm writing about love. I'm writing
about my father. I'm writing about the light."

Walking the Dog

Blackdog and I, we've slowed down.
We take our evening walk down the alley leisurely,
having learned at last to go easy, to stop and smell
roses, or garbage cans, scents of the city.
It pains Blackdog to walk, arthritic hips gone awry,
and pains me to watch her hobble,
so we just go slow, old Labrador leading the way
or lagging behind, the two of us looking around
and finding ourselves in the last chapter
of our life together. It's always sad
to finish a long, well-written book,
pondering the last paragraphs,
the final few sentences,
then sighing
over the period
at the end of the story.
The leash now slack in my hand,
I admire Blackdog's eyes, sad and wise.
Our alley is beautiful with graffiti,
potholes, broken fences, that patch of sky
edged with clouds. At the alley's end,
we hesitate before turning back toward home.
Walking slowly, I tell Blackdog that when I finish a book,
I am a better person for having read every word.
I thank her for the treasure
she has buried like a bone in my heart.

The River of Time

It's raining,
so for my night class
I pass out a poem about the boatman
who ferries souls across the river of time,
a poem I've copied
from the original Latin
by hand in ink
on paper I've made from a pulp
of daylilies, iris leaves,
and (my secret ingredient)
obituaries.
I instruct the students,
as I rise ceremoniously,
to please translate the lines,
if not into English,
then into any language they choose,
French or German,
or perhaps a language of their own invention,
reminding them
as I step backward,
the doorknob in my hand, the door opening,
thunder rumbling in the night,
to seize the day—
finally excusing myself with a slight bow
as I take the boatman's hand
and step
into the little boat that waits
bobbing on the river
outside the classroom door.
The rain comes harder

and the boatman,
huddled under his black cowl,
sets burning eyes on the distant shore.
I rest my hand
on the boatman's shoulder,
and as we float downriver
toward the unseen world across the water,
I turn and bid my students farewell—
waving my scarf,
blowing kisses,
crying out as I am ferried away,
Au revoir, arrivederci, vaya con Dios!

My Samovar!

Whatever happened to the samovar
my wife purchased
at a flea market in Cleveland
and presented to me on my birthday
with wishes that I should live
forever? Ornate, sumptuous,
the samovar commanded attention
and fetched compliments for its beauty—
it *wouldn't* have simply vanished.
Tall, round, vase-shaped,
a copper-and-brass work of art
in the dining room—entire chapters
of life I wrote at its table—
brewing black tea and pouring it
from the jeweled and gilded teapot
that sat atop the inscribed kettle
like a little god
that invited not only the body
but also the soul to partake.
Medicinal and therapeutic,
the samovar guided us
through each day, each season,
insisting we slow down,
live slowly.
Mint, jasmine, orange peel,
rose, linden flowers, lemon,
tea with champagne,
tea with blueberries and currants,
honey tea, peach tea, tea with apples—
I drank them all

from a tulip-shaped tea-glass.
My wife preferred a white porcelain cup.
Our ceremonies were quiet, serene,
characteristically Japanese,
or ritualistic and proper
in the English manner;
but sometimes
like Turks or Russians
we were unrestrained and expansive,
everybody talking as music played
and the children ran around
eating cookies and cakes.
I must admit it is strange
to lose a samovar.
If I could lose *it,*
what else at this moment
might be slipping away?
Without my seeing or knowing,
what else like my beloved samovar
has gone missing
and now is lost, never to return?

Promiscuity

I can fall in love with almost any book,
whether it's *Le rouge et le noir* by Stendhal,
or *Nightwood* by Djuna Barnes,
a book T.S. Eliot claimed only sensibilities
trained on poetry can wholly appreciate.
In Rome I walk into any restaurant
and feel at home, my eyes delighted
by whatever dish appears before me—
steak with fresh twigs of rosemary
and lathered in Colonnata lard,
cut with a knife so sharp I want to steal it,
or *branzino* with lemon and herbs,
that delicious silver fish with its tiny bones,
the eye flirtatiously winking.
Some days when my wife is at work,
I open her closet, take the stops
from her perfume bottles, and inhale
each fragrance to loose memories
of lifting her hand to my lips
and kissing the pulsing wrist's pale skin
before lifting her long black hair
to linger on the scent gracing her neck.
My heart entertains delicious thoughts
as I sit by the window in lace-filtered light,
reading first a poem by my sweetheart Emily,
then an intensely noble, heartrending passage
on what it means to be an artist and in love,
from the notebooks of Rainer Maria Rilke.
Tell me, how on earth could I select just one
flower or gem or distant star to call my own?

How would it even be possible to proclaim
this day is better than all the other days,
when even the years of suffering felt sweet?

Marriage

We walk under cedars
to the lake's edge
and undress,
separately,
in silence,
then wade
slowly into cool,
black water
as one might
enter sleep,
unwilling to let
go of the hand
one loves,
yet letting go
and swimming
toward
the stillness
of the deep,
each of us alone
in our lake of dreams,
minds floating
like clouds or stars
on the still, black water.

Prayer

Let's rest by the lake.
Let's sit by the water's edge together.
Let's sit quietly, at peace.
Let's rest in the silence.
Let's note the mirror stillness of the lake.
Let's note the splendor of heaven.
Let's remember love.
Let's lie down in the grass.
Let's want for nothing.
Let's shine as brightly as the shining sun.
Let's be beautiful. Let's be beautiful together.
Let's speak with pure tongues.
Let's comfort one another.
Let's believe once again in goodness and mercy.

The Silver Painting

I set up my easel on the mountain path.
Opened my box of paints.
I'd hoped the distant peak's simple outline
would shape my small canvas
and the rest would come easily—
the joy of brushstroke and harmony of color.
Then came a lone cloud, swiftly followed
by a fleet of clouds that obscured the summit
and hills below. I hurriedly painted *The Mountain,*
which soon became *Mountain Veiled with Clouds.*
The mountain became ephemeral and vague
in the cryptic rain. The canvas darkened.
I opened my umbrella. I took my smallest brush
and lost myself painting lightning spikes of silver rain.
When I finally looked up, the sky had cleared,
now pink and sapphire. I broke down
my easel and paint box, closed my umbrella,
and walked the steep path down. I put my things
in the car and looked one last time at the canvas
to see what it had become—rain falling
on the black ribbon of a river at night.
Or rain streaking a thousand city windows.
Or my grandmother in a blue silk dressing gown,
sleepily unpinning and dreamily brushing
her loosed gray hair with a long-handled silver brush.

The Arrangement

From the garden's thick-blooming weeping cherry
I snipped three branches—
heavy laden, the white of snow.

Lovely on the table in a glass vase,
the slender branches spiraled high,
reaching upward,

yet something in the arrangement was missing,
some ephemeral grace or affection,
some mystery.

"It's my lack of art," I thought,
but then dusk came
and I found you beside the flowers,

sitting with your pen,
searching for the right words
for the sympathy note you were writing.

Impermanence

Three painters painting a cottage across the street
climb down ladders and clean their brushes,
then sit together on the grass in the cool shade
and eat their lunch in the quiet August noon.
The postman parks his white Jeep on the corner,
swings open the door, pours coffee from a thermos,
unwraps a sandwich he eats slowly, then sits
for twenty minutes doing nothing. Next door,
the music teacher helps a boy carry a cello
down steep front steps to a waiting car,
then absentmindedly bends to pick a few weeds
from a parched garden that is mostly weeds.
Standing under a tall spruce clearing my head
of ten thousand disappointed desires and dreams,
I think of nothing but the holy things here today—
painters, cello, ladders, the mailman's leather pouch,
rooftops, weeds, a mother driving away with her boy,
and the small white cottage that tomorrow will be red.

I didn't expect my father

to walk through the wall
at midnight when I was
sitting in the wing chair
which my mother insisted
I take after he died because
she thought a wing chair
in my study with a tall lamp
would be perfect for one
who sits up late reading
and thinking about the dead
which is what I was doing
when my father arrived and
I rose—as he'd taught me—
and offered him his chair.

My Mother's Visit

My mother was the first pianist I ever heard.
She played hymns. All through childhood
I was spellbound by her gift, her virtuosity.
Now I welcome her to my house,
show her the grand piano,
and lift the lid to its full height and glory.
I ask her to join me on the black bench.
At ninety she is striking, her blue eyes
like summer, her quick smile beguiling.
She is smartly dressed in black slacks,
cream turtleneck, and powder-blue blazer.
Her white hair is her glory, like high clouds
or the dazzling white of sunlit snow.
Sitting together, I tell her my secret:
I've learned to play.
But as I open the hymnal
to "Come, Thou Fount of Every Blessing,"
she sees my hands hesitate.
To give me time,
she, a lifelong Presbyterian,
touches the author's name in the hymnal
and tells a story. The hymn was written
in London in the 1700s. She says back then
London was like Babylon, and Robert Robinson
was a lost soul, a hooligan, who had no need of God
and toughed it out on the streets. That's where the line
"Jesus sought me when a stranger" comes from, she says,
and the way she levels her eyes makes me think
she is talking about my own wayward youth.
I take a breath, lift my hands,

and notes flower forth,
harmony and melody in accord.
On the seventh measure
I stumble and lose my way.
My mother instructs me.
"Feel the music," she says.
"Feel the music and let it
flow through your body."
Emily Dickinson advised
to keep the soul's door ajar.
Perhaps that is what I'm doing,
trying so late in life
to learn how to play,
letting her teach me.

Bedlam

People vanish. They lose their minds,
and their loved ones no longer find them
hiding behind those empty eyes.
In old London the mad were taken
to Bethlem Royal Hospital,
which in their thick accents
the citizens called "Bedlam."
Bedlam was a place where,
according to the mayor in 1450,
one would find "many men
that be fallen out of their wits,"
an infamous place known for cruelty—
chains and manacles, freezing baths
and bleedings, solitary cells for the purpose
of depletion and purgation.
If it were 1750 and I sought amusement,
the tour book says I could pay a penny
and go inside and walk the wards for the titillation
of seeing lunatics starving on their filthy mats.
Foucault in his *History of Madness* claims
96,000 visitors a year. I shiver. The day is cold.
Walking in Bishopsgate, chilled from the damp,
I imagine standing outside the tall iron fence
of the original, long-lost building.
I count the barred windows
and note the glass's reflected waterfalls of light,
as if there were still hope for desolate humankind.
In my mind I see the wide gardens
and hear a cacophony of birdsong,
London's birds hidden in nests in the winter branches.

"Bare ruined choirs, where late the sweet birds sang."
I open the gate to go in. The iron hinge creaks…
That someone has come,
after all these years, startles the birds.
Hundreds lift from the trees and take flight
as if all the birds had suddenly come to their senses
and remembered they had wings.

Socks

After many long years, I finally
finished the book I was writing.
I wondered what to do next.
My whole day ahead of me,
I decided to tidy the sock drawer,
an impossible jumble of lone
survivors and mismatched pairs.
I pulled the big drawer out
and emptied onto the bed
a small mountain of socks.
I began to arrange by color—
the red ones I bought in Rome
at Gammarelli's, the pink ones
found in the Paris street market.
I began lining up all my socks,
much as I do with my poems,
and tenderly folding them one
on top of the other in pairs.
I scolded myself for neglecting
just how important socks are
to a poet walking the path, how
necessary to cushion and adorn
the two feet that carry the heart
up and down the ladders of heaven.
Slowly, I lined the waiting drawer
like a rainbow, from yellow to
purple, noting the black socks
ran on and on like an ellipsis…
Then I put the drawer back.
It was only noon. The room

was bright. All morning
I'd worked in my bare feet
and now my feet were cold.
I wanted to lie on the bed
and daydream, but not before
I thought to put on a fresh
pair of soft white socks,
warm white socks with soles
so pristine and unsullied
it was as though they had
never been anywhere.

Midnight

I no longer have the luxury
of breaking down as I did in my youth.
I have to be here at night to tuck in my daughter
and sit with her in the dark.
I tell her I am glad she is exactly who she is,
a gift, a joy,
and that it is an honor
to be her father, to bless her
and pray a hedge of protection around her
as she falls asleep.
I do the same with my son William,
who is wise and knows how to make me laugh.
He sprawls long-limbed across his bed,
tired and drained from days of soccer,
and when I enter his room
he rolls over, knowing I will rub his sore back.
His breathing deepens.
He begins to dream.
What a blessing—
to kiss my children at day's end.
Midnight finds me talking
with my eldest, the young scholar at his desk
still at work on his computer.
In the big black office chair I gave him,
he turns toward me, his eyes shining.
I tell him what I've told you,
how lucky I am, how grateful.
I rest my hand on his shoulder and say good night,
as if we were "men that strove with gods"
and did not yield.

Standing in the doorway
I tell him that's a line from Tennyson's "Ulysses,"
then cross the hall to my room,
where a lamp is still burning and my wife is waiting
for me to take her hand, as I do each night,
and thank her and thank her for everything.

Washing Your Feet

I began with your ankle,
holding your heel in my hand
and ladling warm water
that spilled over your arches
and down between your toes,
before softly splashing
into the wooden bowl.
I rubbed the steel cable
of the Achilles tendon,
the two small mountains
of the ankle, the dull pad
of the heel, then washed
the sole, the foot's white
underbelly, and the shy
instep, tender as the palm
of your hand. My fingers
scrubbed your modest toes,
my thumb rubbed each nail,
pouring clean water now
and again from the ladle.
I don't know exactly how
Jesus did it in the upper room,
but like him I was kneeling,
and when I was finished
washing your left foot
and drying it with a towel,
I set your foot very gently down,
then turned to wash your right.

Throne of Dreams

When my retina tore,
my right eye filled with blood.
The doctor who promised to cure my blindness
told me, "You are not to read or write,"
fearing the back-and-forth eye movement
would cause permanent damage
and loss of vision.
I was to sit and not move,
to sleep upright at night,
to be perfectly still.
This I did for forty days.
I found my house had many chairs—
the gray chair in the den with the armrest
where with closed eyes
I could meditate for hours,
and the green wrought-iron chair
in the garden where I listened to birds,
wind high in the maples,
and the dull clapping of bamboo wind chimes.
By the fireplace my father's tall wingback chair
helped me remember how quiet
he became at the end of his life,
how peaceful,
an old soldier reminding me
they also serve who only stand and wait.
And at night there was
at the foot of the bed where my wife slept,
the small white sofa.
I put a hassock under my feet
and sat up straight to sleep

in the valley between two mountains
of pillows and blankets,
a makeshift throne of dreams
soft as a cloud drifting higher and higher.
"Don't read or write?"
I had repeated back to the doctor,
that first day in his office.
He didn't know what he was saying,
but he also didn't know
I am blessed to have a daughter.
She carefully taps each line I say
into a silver laptop computer,
then reads everything slowly back to me,
making corrections and suggesting changes,
sage little improvements she insists upon
before letting the poem go
alone into the wide darkness and gloom
to sing and shine and share its joy.

Paradise

I cannot tell you how much I love
going for a run with my boys,
two young men taller than I,
swift as gazelles, strong as lions.
We run a paved trail near our house
that winds through the forest preserve
and my boys go slow and easy
as I huff and wheeze beside them,
the trees nodding in the breeze
as we cross the little bridge
or run single file to let cyclists pass.
The years when they were little,
I stopped running—my knees
and back couldn't take it. Before,
I'd run for distance every day,
the miles ahead an open invitation
I could never resist. I tell my boys—
bragging as I struggle to keep up—
"In high school I could run
close to a four-minute mile,"
and as we turn at last for home,
I do my utmost to show the old form—
arms pumping a heartbeat rhythm,
back straight, breathing steady.
But sometimes my sons need to run.
They promise to meet me up ahead,
then take off flying like two jets
and disappear around the bend.
Alone in the forest preserve,
I listen to the swift little stream,

how the water is a clear music,
like the wind rushing through trees.
Slowing down, I think this is how
it will be, running in Elysium,
where everyone is young and swift,
where the meadows are like bliss
and the paths ahead shine, calling us, breathless.

Another Unwritten Excerpt from My Daughter's Diary: "The Waste Land" and My Father

The windows are bright with English sky,
and the light bathes my father's face,
his eyes closed as if listening to the sunshine.
At midafternoon the pub is quiet, almost reverent.
My father excuses himself and goes to the loo.
The *Collected Poems,* upturned on the scarred wooden table,
invites my fingers to examine the smooth cloth
and gold-embossed initials—T.S.E.—shining
in the otherwise unembellished black cover.
My father returns with a fresh pint for him
and another cookie for me.
He opens the book and reads at random.
It makes no difference where the book opens
or what line he reads—if the poetry is true, he says,
then every word is efficacious and edifying,
enlightening and enriching. He takes a sip of bitter
and reads: "I said to my soul, be still,
and let the dark come upon you."
No one talks about the soul anymore, my father says—
people are too afraid; but I tell him I grew strong
with a father who honored the soul and its longing.
In the London pub I tell him I am happy,
and also how happy I am for him.
The "end of the endless journey to no end."
My father smiles at me, bows his head in thanks,
and closes the book. He directs my eyes
to the window and says there will be fog this evening.
The fog will come from the sea and drift up the Thames.
It will be a good night to go wandering—

we will disappear down narrow streets,
losing ourselves in London's dark alleys,
our shadows falling somewhere "between the idea
And the reality." Sounds good to me, I say.
Then, while he sips the last of his bitter,
I open the book to the end of "The Waste Land"
and read aloud the last line—
"Shantih   shantih   shantih."

Rubble and Ruins

This morning I rose early to write,
looking for signs of life amid the carnage,
digging and chipping through the rubble and ruins
with my pen. The house was hushed;
the hours slipped by in an instant.
At noon I left home to give a talk
to a friend's literature class at the university.
I'd been asked to explain what poetry is,
and that's what I was thinking about
as I drove down Lake Shore Drive.
The first red and gold leaves were falling,
drifting and swirling across the road,
and the October sky was sunny and clear,
the lake's calm water freckled
with light diamonds.
On the radio,
I heard Patrick Modiano had won
the Nobel Prize in Literature.
Reading from his script, the announcer said
the French author's themes
were time, memory, and identity.
What other themes are there, I wondered.
Modiano writes about the Nazi occupation of France.
As the radio says, we look back through a glass darkly
and think about the past.
I write about London in the years after the War,
when orphans lived on rations
and tried to be happy,
walking among the wreckage and bombed-out buildings.
I have distant and elusive memories

of the house my family lived in,
and now and again
I catch sight of my mother in her tweed coat
or my father in his uniform,
spying each out of the corner of my eye,
the way, when driving,
I spot clouds mounting on the lake's far horizon.

The Fortune Cookie

At five o'clock on a long-ago Tuesday
I met my friend Mark at Piccadilly.
He'd been in the Scottish Highlands;
I'd been in Paris. He still talks about
how strange it was to be in another country
and see my young face appearing
like an apparition out of the crowds.
Under Cupid's aimed bow and arrow,
we stood with our arms around the girls
we loved back then, as we asked a polite
English punk with spiked blue hair
to take our snapshot. In the evening
a light rain was falling as the four of us
walked through Soho, looking for a place to eat.
We turned a corner and there was Lee Ho Fook's,
the Chinese restaurant Warren Zevon sings about
in "Werewolves of London." At dinner Mark
tied together everything under the sun—
Virginia Woolf walking into the river, the lions
of heraldry, the tragic introduction of the tea bag
into English culture, the lofty oculus in the Reading
Room of the British Library. We all agreed:
we do not wander aimlessly in this world,
but rather everything calls us to the ground of our being.
Rivers and lions. Books and arrows.
The hopes of youth have vanished
and three decades have passed
since that night. Yet still I carry in my wallet—
as if it were a talisman or the tiniest poem ever written—
the little strip of paper with its words of wisdom:
"Everything is not yet lost."

The Land of Milk and Honey

Finally I just decided to go,
to follow the wind wherever
the wind wished to take me.
I drove my old blue car north
into wild, wooded country,
an old-growth forest
of white pines and larches,
green ash and northern red oak.
I pulled to the side of the road
where a clear stream rushed
like a song freely spilling
over moss-covered rocks.
I couldn't have been happier,
but happiness was not the plan,
the wind was the plan. And so
I did not set up camp—
I drove. The road narrowed
and came to an end.
I left the car beneath a cliff
and walked on. A basalt
escarpment reared before me.
I hiked along the crest,
using a twisted limb of cedar
for my walking staff.
But that high up, the wind,
which had its ancient origin
in a country far to the north,
was now furor and tumult,
a whirlwind blowing
and whipping in every direction.

I shrugged off my backpack
and rested between boulders
worn smooth over millennia
by that same wind. My eyes
looked down on open country
and endless sky, a red sun
setting over a distant river
ablaze in the dying light.
Then the wind died down.
The first stars appeared.
A cold night was coming
and everything became still.
From the mountaintop, I saw
that I was at peace right here
and could die happy this night,
never crossing to the other side.
Beyond the river it was already dark.
It was as if I were looking down
from the heights of Mount Nebo
on the land of milk and honey.

For we are here for but a moment,
strangers in the land as our fathers were before us;
our days on earth are like a shadow,
gone so soon, without a trace.

Acknowledgments

AGNI: "At the Carnavalet and the Cognacq-Jay"

American Journal of Poetry: "Prayer"

Anchor: "Scarlet Fever"

Apple Valley Review: "The Hidden Meadow"

Asheville Poetry Review: "Rilke and Rodin"

Blue Earth Review: "Her Majesty," "The Honeymoon," "Throne of Dreams"

Boaat: "The French Word for 'Sky'"

Broad River Review: "Portraits"

Cape Rock: "Midnight"

Chiron Review: "Fog," "Nova Scotia," "Walking Miracle"

Cloudbank: "Socks"

Communion: "Hearts"

Cossack Review: "Rubble and Ruins"

Cultural Weekly: "Bedlam," "The Black Raincoat," "Canto 34," "Canto 35," "Canto 36," "Canto 37," "Canto 38," "Canto 39," "Canto 40," "Check-up," "The End is Here, Almost," "Hallmark," "I Call My Mother Once a Week," "Lost," "The Messengers," "Salt," "Shoes"

Door is a Jar: "The Biscuit Tin," "Help"

Escape into Life: "The Blue Notebook," "Brussels," "The Coffin Shop," "Gliders," "Long Journey," "Mars," "Nocturne," "Promiscuity," "Typewriters," "Washing Your Feet"

Fact of the Universe: "Blue," "The City in the Clouds," "The Light," "Quest," "Ravenous," "Small Talk"

The Feast: "The Silver Painting"

Fifth Wednesday Journal: "Another Unwritten Excerpt from My Daughter's Diary: 'The Waste Land' and My Father," "Canto 1," "Canto 4," "Canto 5," "Canto 7," "Canto 9," "Canto 12," "Canto 16," "Canto 19," "Dickens's House," "The Garden," "My Samovar!" "Unwritten Excerpt from My Daughter's Diary: 'The Hollow Men' and My Father"

FR&D: "Canto 20"

GFT Press: "Canto 2," "Canto 3," "Canto 6," "Canto 8," "Canto 10," "Canto 11," "Canto 13," "Canto 14," "Canto 15," "Canto 17," "Canto 18," "Canto 22," "Canto 25," "Canto 26," "The Flight to Madrid," "Madeleines"

Great River Review: "Canto 21," "Canto 23," "Canto 24"

Hamilton Stone Review: "Dreaming in the Language of Angels," "The Drunken Boat," "*The Gift*," "The Sky," "Water Lilies, Green Reflections"

The Hiram Review: "Walking the Dog"

Hampden-Sydney Poetry Review: "Rainstorm"

Image: "Church Bells," "English Lit," "The Manifestation," "My Mother's Visit," "Pont des Arts," "Prodigal"

Kentucky Review: "The Land of Milk and Honey," "The Used-Book Store," "The Windmill"

KYSO Flash: "The Philosophers' Banquet: A Cento Sonnet"

L'Éphémère Review: "Directions," "Margins"

Literature and Belief: "The Aladdin Blue Flame Heater," "Bread Street," "Covent Garden," "The Eighth Day," "Hearing Aids," "The History of the Desk," "The Taj Mahal," "Tin Cans," "Vertigo," "Villiers Street"

The Meadow: "Marriage," "On the Run"

Narrative: "Faith," "TWA Flight 800"

New Madrid: "The Coronation"

ONTHEBUS: "Eggplant," "January Night"

Plume: "Blue Plaques"

Poet Lore: "Afterward," "Attics," "Broom," "The Call," "The Chair," "Freud's Glasses," "Gardener," "Postcards Tucked in the Dresser's Mirror"

Poetry Daily: "Waterloo"

Poetry South: "Bedtime Story," "Cake," "Canto 27," "Canto 28," "Canto 29," "Goodbye," "Home," "Rhapsody," "The Tantalus," "Tribulation"

Potomac Review: "Blue Stars," "The Egg"

Rock & Sling: "Paradise"

Serving House Journal: "The Leather Flask"

Smartish Pace: "The River of Time"

Star 82: "Omnia Omnibus Ubique," "Winston Churchill," "Wordsworth's Barn"

The Tishman Review: "The Home Office," "Sherlock Holmes"

Two Cities Review: "The Fortune Cookie"

Under a Warm Green Linden: "The Camino," "Here on Planet Earth," "I didn't expect my father," "Impermanence," "The Nomenclature of Color," "The Silver Cord"

upstreet: "The Bombed-out Library," "Standing in the Dark by My Mother's Narrow Bed," "Waterloo"

U.S. 1 Worksheets: "The Races"

Valley Voices: "Canto 30," "Canto 31," "Canto 32," "Canto 33"

Wallace Stevens Journal: "The Arrangement"

West Texas Literary Review: "After the Rain," "Andrew and William," "The Parable"

About the Author

Richard Jones is the author of a number of books of poetry, including *Country of Air, The Blessing: New and Selected Poems, Apropos of Nothing,* and *The King of Hearts.* He is also the award-winning editor of *Poetry East* and over the last four decades has curated its many anthologies, such as *The Last Believer in Words, Bliss, Wider than the Sky,* and *Paris.* He lives in Illinois with his family.

Copper Canyon Press and the author gratefully acknowledge the Vincentian Endowment Foundation and the University Research Council of DePaul University for their generous support.

Poetry is vital to language and living. Since 1972, Copper Canyon Press has published extraordinary poetry from around the world to engage the imaginations and intellects of readers, writers, booksellers, librarians, teachers, students, and donors.

WE ARE GRATEFUL FOR THE MAJOR SUPPORT PROVIDED BY:

THE PAUL G. ALLEN
FAMILY FOUNDATION

 amazon *literary partnership*

 the**point** envision·enact·evolve

 4 CULTURE

 golden lasso

Lannan

 ART WORKS. | National Endowment for the Arts arts.gov

 A& OFFICE OF ARTS & CULTURE SEATTLE

 WASHINGTON STATE ARTS COMMISSION

TO LEARN MORE ABOUT UNDERWRITING
COPPER CANYON PRESS TITLES,
PLEASE CALL 360-385-4925 EXT. 103

WE ARE GRATEFUL FOR THE MAJOR SUPPORT PROVIDED BY:

Anonymous

Jill Baker and Jeffrey Bishop

Donna and Matt Bellew

John Branch

Diana Broze

Sarah and Tim Cavanaugh

Janet and Les Cox

Mimi Gardner Gates

Linda Gerrard and Walter Parsons

Gull Industries Inc. on behalf of
  Ruth and William True

The Trust of Warren A. Gummow

Steven Myron Holl

Phil Kovacevich and Eric Wechsler

Lakeside Industries Inc.
  on behalf of Jeanne Marie Lee

Maureen Lee and Mark Busto

Rhoady Lee and Alan Gartenhaus

Ellie Mathews and Carl Youngmann
  as The North Press

Anne O'Donnell and John Phillips

Petunia Charitable Fund and
  adviser Elizabeth Hebert

Suzie Rapp and Mark Hamilton

Emily and Dan Raymond

Jill and Bill Ruckelshaus

Cynthia Lovelace Sears and
  Frank Buxton

Kim and Jeff Seely

Dan Waggoner

Barbara and Charles Wright

The dedicated interns and
  faithful volunteers of
  Copper Canyon Press

The Chinese character for poetry is made up of two parts: "word"
and "temple." It also serves as pressmark for
Copper Canyon Press.

The poems are set in Minion. Display type is Futura.
Book design and composition by Phil Kovacevich.

CPSIA information can be obtained
at www.ICGtesting.com
Printed in the USA
LVHW01s0248080518
576341LV00003B/3/P